"From her vast experience working as a professional medium, Hollister has provided an amazing and user-friendly guide that answers every question you would ever have about mediumship and the afterlife. Through personal experiences, stories, and exercises, she helps to alleviate any doubts and fears about death and the soul's journey, and just as important, reveals how we can connect with those ancestors."

—Dr. Steven Farmer, author of *Animal Spirit Guides*
and *Sacred Ceremony*

***

"I've personally experienced Hollister Rand's gift and am consistently amazed by her ability to share spirit messages with accuracy, open heartedness, and compassion. In her new book, *Everything You Wanted to Know about the Afterlife*, the spirit wisdom she shares can bring healing to the pain of loss and peace to a broken heart. I highly recommend the book to everyone who seeks answers and insights from the invisible realm."

—James F. Twyman, *New York Times* bestselling author
and peace troubadour

***

"I have seen Hollister in action and have seen how she has changed lives by her truest gift of communicating with the other side. In fact, I had a one-on-one session with her that brought me so much clarity that it's still benefiting me in ways I can't even put into words. Her new book, *Everything You Wanted to Know About the Afterlife but Were Afraid to Ask* is a must read! Her insight will bring peace to heart and a calm knowing to your soul."

—Glenn Scarpelli, owner/producer of Sedona NOW TV
and actor on *One Day At A Time*

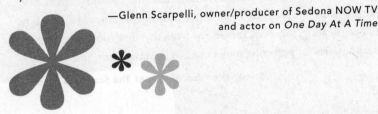

"Hollister is a gifted medium, a great writer, and a very special person. All three aspects shine brightly in this engaging and inspiring book. If you are interested in learning about the afterlife as experienced by a skilled and thoughtful medium, you will love this book."

—Gary E. Schwartz, PhD, senior professor and director of the Laboratory for Advances in Consciousness and Health at the University of Arizona, and author of *The Afterlife Experiments, The Sacred Promise,* and *Super Synchronicity*

***

"One need not believe in anything more than hope to benefit from this wonderful book. Hollister Rand is a master of unraveling life's great mysteries and healing broken hearts."

—Dr. Ken Druck, bestselling author of *The Real Rules of Life*

***

"Meet your personal guide to the afterlife! Medium Hollister Rand shares everything you need to know about the spirit world in a fresh, fun way that dispels all those dusty superstitions and myths. If you've always wanted to connect with loved ones in spirit and really understand what's going on 'beyond the veil,' Hollister shines her light and leads the way."

—Sara Wiseman, author of *Messages from the Divine*

***

"Hollister's knowledgeable, quirky, experienced, and often funny voice lends itself to a book that is both easy to read and yet very deep at the same time. By using her vast past experiences and readings as the platform, Hollister zones in on each answer in a way that everyone can relate to. Hollister has left no stone unturned!"

—Danielle McKinnon, intuitive animal communicator and author of *Animal Lessons*

Everything You Wanted to Know about the Afterlife*

Everything You Wanted to Know about the Afterlife*

Explained by
Hollister Rand

* BUT WERE AFRAID TO ASK

ATRIA PAPERBACK
New York London Toronto Sydney New Delhi

BEYOND WORDS
Hillsboro, Oregon

ATRIA PAPERBACK

An Imprint of Simon & Schuster, Inc.
1230 Avenue of the Americas
New York, NY 10020

BEYOND WORDS

8427 N.E. Cornell Road, Suite 500
Hillsboro, Oregon 97124-9808
503-531-8700 / 503-531-8773 fax
www.beyondword.com

Managing Editor: Lindsay S. Easterbrooks-Brown
Editor: Emily Han
Copyeditor: Jennifer Weaver-Neist
Proofreader: Linda Meyer
Design: Sara E. Blum
Composition: William H. Brunson Typography Services

First Beyond Words/Atria paperback edition May 2020

For information about special discounts for bulk purchases, please contact Simon & Schuster Special Sales at 1-866-506-1949 or business@simonandschuster.com.

The Simon & Schuster Speakers Bureau can bring authors to your live event. For more information or to book an event, contact Simon & Schuster Speakers Bureau at 1-866-248-3049 or visit our website at www.simonspeakers.com.

Manufactured in the United States of America

10   9   8   7   6   5   4   3   2   1

Library of Congress Cataloging-in-Publication Data

Names: Rand, Hollister, author.
Title: Everything you wanted to know about the afterlife but were afraid to ask / explained by Hollister Rand.
Description: First Beyond Words/Atria paperback edition. | New York : Atria Paperback ; Hillsboro, Oregon : Beyond Words, 2020. | Includes bibliographical references. | Summary: "Over the many years of her mediumship, Hollister Rand has worked with tens of thousands of people with questions about and for their loved ones who have passed beyond the veil. Now, Hollister has brought her popular online and live Q&A sessions to the page. Hollister's warm tone, sense of humor, and authenticity regarding her own spiritual journey will guide you through the ins and outs of the afterlife, providing comfort, clarity, and some laughs along the way"— Provided by publisher.
Identifiers: LCCN 2019055494 (print) | LCCN 2019055495 (ebook) | ISBN 9781582707280 (paperback) | ISBN 9781982135539 (ebook)
Subjects: LCSH: Future life. | Spiritualism.
Classification: LCC BF1311.F8 R28 2020 (print) | LCC BF1311.F8 (ebook) | DDC 133.901/3—dc23
LC record available at https://lccn.loc.gov/2019055494
LC ebook record available at https://lccn.loc.gov/2019055495

The corporate mission of Beyond Words Publishing, Inc.: *Inspire to Integrity*

To my father, Francis H. Gierisch,
whose love of nature taught me to thrive
in a landscape alien to my soul.

Thank you, Dad.

In the end, the only events worth telling are those in which the imperishable world erupted into this transitory world.

Carl Jung at the age of eighty-two

CHAPTER 4: LIFE IN THE AFTERLIFE

24. Do spirits need to learn how to connect with us, in the physical realm? 90

25. Are there seasons/climates in the afterlife? 94

26. Do spirits have jobs? 100

27. Do spirits go on vacation? 103

28. Do spirits have to eat? 104

29. Do soldiers in spirit talk about combat and its effect on them and their families? 107

CHAPTER 5: AFTERLIFE RELATIONSHIPS

30. Do spirits know how much we love and miss them? 112

31. Do spirits still feel love for us? 115

32. Does romantic love exist in the afterlife? 117

33. Do spirits get jealous? 120

34. Can spirits intervene on our behalf? 124

35. What is the best way to honor the memory of a loved one in spirit? 128

36. What is the difference between guides and angels? 132

37. How can I meet my spirit guide? 137

CHAPTER 6: THE LANGUAGE OF SPIRITS

38. Is there a "veil" that separates the living from the dead? 144

39. Is it true that spirits can visit us in dreams? 146

40. What are the signs that a spirit is present? 150

41. Can spirits hear our thoughts? 157

42. Do spirits come to us as insects and animals? 161

43. Do flowers have a special significance to spirits? 163

44. Is it easier to feel the presence of spirits when near water? 166

45. Is it possible to communicate with our ancestors? 169

CHAPTER 7: FOR THE LOVE OF ANIMALS

46. Can the spirits of pets communicate through a medium? 176

47. Do pets reincarnate? 182

48. Do animals in spirit help us in our lives? 185

CHAPTER 8: SPIRITED OCCASIONS

49. Do spirits honor holiday traditions? 192

50. Do the holidays draw spirits closer to us? 196

51. How can I manage during the holidays when missing
someone I love? 199

CHAPTER 9: THE BIG QUESTIONS

52. Do spirits tell you if there's a God? 204

53. What does it mean to be spiritually connected? 207

54. Is it true that our experiences on Earth are a sort of
life school? 210

55. Do spirits agree with us about what is good and
what is bad? 213

56. Are soul mates a real thing? 216

57. If my loved ones reincarnate before I die, will we miss
seeing one another in the afterlife? 223

58. Is it possible to love again when you've lost everyone
you love? 228

59. Are spirits aware of disasters, including ecological ones? 232

60. Can spirits help change my destiny? 234

61. Can we escape our karma? 237

62. Can spirits help us find peace after loss? 240

Conclusion 245

Acknowledgments 247

Appendix: Q&A Cross-References 249

Notes 251

Recommended Resources 253

About the Author 257

Note from the Author

This book includes actual encounters with spirits and with people in the physical/Earth realm (loved ones, private clients, readers, workshop attendees, and so on). In writing about these experiences, the names and details have been changed to protect the identities of those involved. Spirit messages could not be presented in their entirety and verbatim; they have been edited and consolidated for the purposes of this book. Examples, exercises, and thematic refrains may have been presented in my previous book, magazine articles, workshops, and online events.

Note from the Publisher

Dear Reader,

Richard and I are so pleased to be able to bring this material to you, and we consider it divinely inspired: had we not met Hollister Rand in person, it never would have happened.

We first witnessed Hollister's amazing abilities at an afterlife conference in Portland, Oregon. There were five hundred attendees in the room, and it was streamed to thousands more. In the crowd were mothers, fathers, sisters, brothers, friends, and lovers—all hoping to reconnect with a loved one who had crossed over. It was an atmosphere of hope, sadness, anxiety, and curiosity, all rolled into one.

As Hollister took the stage, she asked the crowd to write on a piece of paper any question they had about the afterlife or about loved ones who had passed. When the questions were gathered, they were placed in a large wicker basket and brought to her. Hollister took a breath, put her hand in the basket, read the question aloud, and the healing began.

There were more questions than time permitted in that one-and-a-half-hour session; however, we saw tears of joy, moments of great comfort, and profound healings. What was surprising to us is that even though not all questions had been taken out of the basket, it seemed that each person in the audience had received the answer they so desired.

We witnessed visits from loved ones who had passed due to accidental or intentional overdose, car accidents, illness, or just old age. And as each person received the peace they were looking for, the room felt lighter and lighter. One mother learned her son's death from an overdose was an accident—he didn't really mean to die and leave her. When the mother heard her son's message, she fell to her knees on the floor and wept. It was not something he had done to hurt her, and it was not something for her to feel guilty about anymore. It was simply an accident.

And so began our journey with Hollister. We went to other events and witnessed the same hope and healing.

You see, Hollister doesn't just answer questions; she teaches about the afterlife. She helps us to see a bigger picture painted in words, affirming that we do not cease to exist when we pass this earthly plane; we go on and are never ever left by our loved ones. The ones we love are always near, ready to show us a sign that death does not permanently separate us from them.

After witnessing Hollister's work at many events, we felt it was time to have a session with her to connect with our own family members who had passed. These included a husband who died of brain cancer at forty-nine; a mother who was cold as ice but had softened after transition; and an abusive stepmother in life but an angel in spirit, who wanted to make up for the harm she had caused me at a young age. They all came, and Hollister described each one as though they were standing there in the room.

What happened next was truly remarkable. My daughter and I had some unresolved issues and could not seem to find the connection that love, understanding, and forgiveness can bring to a relationship. Though she had not spoken to me for two years, she called three weeks after the session and then stopped by for a visit. We now speak daily on the phone and have renewed our mother–daughter bond. The spirits had come and brought us back together again.

A while ago, Richard had a session with Hollister; and when his father came into the reading, he said the following to Richard: "I had hopes and dreams for you in this lifetime; however, you did not do any of them. Instead, you exceeded all of them. And now I am learning from you." When he was alive, this all would have seemed a little supernatural to Richard's father, but he now saw there was more to life than he had imagined.

Hollister's questions gave us answers and helped heal our family. It is our sincere wish that as you read *Everything You Wanted to Know about the Afterlife*, your questions will also be answered and you will find peace.

Hollister teaches that we don't really die. Our bodies may be cast away, but our spirits live on, yearning to help those loved ones left behind until they are reunited with us once more. We are so grateful to be working with Hollister as she helps to heal broken hearts and give these answers of hope.

—Michele Ashtiani Cohn,
creative director, Beyond Words Publishing, Inc.

The best
scientists and explorers have
the attributes of kids!
They ask questions and have a
sense of wonder.
They have curiosity—
"Who, what, where, why, when,
and how!"
They never stop asking questions,
and I never stop asking questions,
just like a five-year-old.

Sylvia Alice Earle,
National Geographic
Explorer-in-Residence

Introduction

If what oceanographer Sylvia Earle says is true, then most of us are five years old at heart. We ask questions all day long. We ask to understand who we are and to whom we belong, which explains the popularity of Ancestry.com and 23andMe. We ask our friends what books we should read. We ask Yelp for the best pizzeria in town. We ask Google *everything*. Life is pretty much a Q&A experience—that's just the way we learn.

As a medium, passionate curiosity to know the truth about life and death has fueled my connection with spirits. I have always wanted to know the answers to big questions like "Why are we here?" and practical concerns like "Will I be able to eat what I want in the afterlife?"

As a result of decades of meeting and working with people from all over the world, I've discovered that I'm not the only one with lots of questions about spirits and life after death. Over the years, I've noticed a trend: as more people become familiar with spirit communication, more questions—rather than fewer—are being asked! This ongoing demand for answers has inspired me to present online Q&A forums, write columns for magazines, and host Q&A salon gatherings.

However, oftentimes, following an event, people approach me to ask their questions privately. These questions tend to be the most interesting of all! In other words, the best questions are often from those who are afraid to ask them in front of an audience.

To sidestep this predicament—and to give everyone equal opportunity—I suggest that questions be written down and placed in a basket at my events. I then select a question and provide an answer. What amazes me about this practice is that no matter how much or how little time is allotted, nearly every question gets answered! Due to how frequently this happens, I know spirits guide the Q&A process. Thus, the desire to answer questions in a more expansive way has been growing. Fortunately, my publisher agrees and has asked me to write this book.

∗ ∗ ∗

When it came time to write an outline of the book, I became anxious, as I often do at the outset of any intense endeavor. I asked the spirits if this was the book I should be writing and to give me a sign that I was on the right path. The answer came while I was in San Diego. A dear friend named Tony brought his sister, Linda, to my keynote presentation for New Earth Events. After the event, Tony asked Linda whether she wanted to join us for dinner. She replied, "Better not. I have so many questions to ask that she [meaning me] won't get the chance to eat!" When Tony told me about this conversation, I smiled. This was my "go ahead" from the spirits—a Q&A book about the afterlife is wanted *and* needed!

Before starting to write this book, I took a moment to flip through the pages of my first book, *I'm Not Dead, I'm Different: Kids in Spirit Teach Us about Living a Better Life on Earth*. At first glance, it seemed as though my new book was a complete departure from the first. However, as I started rereading, I was reminded that the very thing that draws me to kids in spirit (and them to me) is a shared curiosity, and a willingness to speak simply and clearly about life and death. Even way back in 2011 (when my first book was published), I felt compelled to answer questions, as each chapter contains a Q&A section. Now, with this new book, I have the opportunity to expand on the Q&A format; and therefore, it is the perfect sequel!

How This Book Works

To keep the book simple and easy to use, the questions are organized by topic. By listing all the questions in the table of contents, your reading experience is flexible, giving you the opportunity to look up your burning questions immediately. For example, if you want to know the answer to "Does romantic love exist in the afterlife?" (Q&A number 32), then you can go directly to that question in chapter 5, "Afterlife Relationships." The book can also be read in short spurts of time, making it suitable for contemplative morning reading, reading during a commute, or even during a lunch break.

Recently, a friend looked over the table of contents and, in surprise, asked rhetorically, "Who knew that I'd want to know the answers to questions I didn't even know to ask?" Well, in my experience with groups, questions always lead to more questions! The same goes for this book: your first question will likely lead to another question, and another, and so on. And before you know it, you will be traveling along your very own journey of discovery. Furthermore, as a reader and a seeker, you can return to this book again and again as a reference. The answers to questions you didn't even know you wanted to ask will be waiting when you're ready.

If the subject of spirit communication is new to you, some words and concepts might be unfamiliar. Words specific to mediumship are defined within the text rather than listed in a separate glossary. This will allow for a smoother reading experience, with no need for turning to another part of the book in the middle of reading an answer.

Exercises and meditations are also included in the main text rather than gathered in an appendix. Hopefully, this will make it easy to incorporate and experience spirit communication while you're reading about it rather than at some time in the future.

Although all the Q&As in this book are interconnected, you will find notes at the end of some Q&As suggesting other related Q&As that I thought would be of interest. This way, a subject can be explored more fully, analogous to searching a subject online and then moving from one article to another. I've also created an appendix ("Q&A Cross-References") with this in mind, to further enhance user friendliness and flow.

This book is intended to be a comfortable and comforting discussion about death and dying—a difficult and, some might say, "taboo" subject. Consider this book to be a conversation with a friend who happens to be a medium, with questions that challenge the fear of the unknown and answers that speak to the heart of loss. Large concepts, like the survival of consciousness beyond death, are explained in a down-to-earth way. This makes the information easily accessible to those who are new to the subject of spirit communication, while providing a depth of understanding for those who are experienced.

While gathering questions for this book, I was disturbed to discover that there is much misinformation passed around about life after death, and about how mediums and spirit communication work. In this book, I bust certain myths and shed light on what some might

consider "the darkest days" that all of us will experience in our lifetimes. Nonetheless, don't think that a book about death and dying has to be depressing! On the contrary, let me assure you that the spirits I encounter treat death in a lighthearted and enlightened way.

Most important, my hope is that this book will serve as a reminder that not only does life continue beyond death, but relationships with loved ones continue as well.

My Mission as a Medium

When I first ventured into spirit communication as a profession, there were times I was called upon to clear houses of ghosts and negative energy. From apparitions floating down a hallway to the haunting of a theater in Los Angeles, I experienced the ugliness of the spirit world. I decided to leave this kind of work behind after a dramatic episode in which the word *rats* was emblazoned in red welts on my right thigh. This occurred even after practicing grounding (consciously anchoring myself energetically to the earth) and protection (the building up of energy around myself like a shield).

Following this episode, I decided to work specifically at the frequency of love and communicate messages from loved ones in spirit. The intention, when connecting with spirits at this frequency, is for messages to be hopeful and helpful. (If you are interested in learning more about how this works, please read Q&A number 3, "Is there a difference between a ghost and a spirit?" in chapter 1, "The Basics.")

It seems important to mention at this point that I stress grounding and protection as an essential practice for mediums, healers, and empaths—and in fact, *anyone* whose openheartedness makes them susceptible to less-than-positive influences. An easy grounding and protection meditation is presented in Q&A number 14, "Is mediumship exhausting work?" in chapter 2, "On Being a Medium." In addition, I created (with inspiration from the spirits) a protection symbol (see below) and placed it at the start of each of the nine chapters, reminding us that as we read and learn about spirits, we do so in an intentionally protected space.

The smallest inner circle represents us—the physical beings living on Earth. The circle surrounding us represents the spirits whose presence supports and guides us. The heart which encompasses these inner circles reminds us that we are connected at and protected by the frequency of love. The wavy broken line represents the frequency of love, as well as a permeable and disappearing divider between life on Earth and in spirit. And finally, the bold outer circle represents the combined protective force of intention and love, which encompasses *all*. Every time you see this symbol, remember: *you are loved and protected*.

Since 1994, I've been dedicated to serving spirits in love by providing messages via a variety of platforms. One type of platform is what I call "gallery-style presentations," which are large gatherings that can have an audience of more than five hundred people in a room and a million or more watching online worldwide. These events, which include afterlife conferences and metaphysical expos, provide an opportunity for people to see how I work. Although the emphasis isn't on providing a personal message for every audience member, the audience can be assured that spirits make good use of the experience—a message for one person can provide insight and comfort to others.

For a more intimate group setting, "spirit circles" have no more than ten sitters, providing the opportunity for each person in the group to receive a personal message. At the same time, each sitter can encounter a variety of other messages and spirits, creating a unique experience.

In case you're wondering what a sitter is, the term derives from the word *séance*, meaning "to sit" in French. A spirit circle is the modern-day version of a séance, so someone who attends a spirit circle is therefore called a sitter. The term séance became less popular as spirit communication moved out of the shadows of heavily draped, candlelit parlors and into the living rooms of today.

Lastly, a private session is the most intimate kind of meeting with a medium, with only one or two sitters and their loved ones (in spirit) involved.

Besides communicating with spirits, I also love sharing what I know about mediumship! This is one of the reasons why people refer to me as "the teaching medium." It is my unshakable belief that *everyone* can connect with and be guided by spirits, and it is my mission to show as many people as possible how to do so. To that end, I've worked in radio and on TV, written books (like this one) and innumerable magazine articles, and taught workshops and online seminars worldwide. Spirit communication is not an exclusive club for the few but, rather, a tool by which we can all enrich our lives.

So, without further ado, I'm delighted to say it is our time to explore the afterlife and spirit communication together. Let the questions and answers begin!

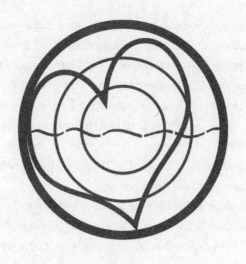

1

The Basics

1. Is there really an afterlife?

This question is a good place to start, though it initially caught me off guard. It was asked during a weeklong Caribbean cruise with a full schedule of metaphysical workshops, and I had assumed that participants had settled the question of an afterlife prior to joining a retreat featuring a medium. Consequently, when I pulled the question out of a basket and read it in front of the enthusiastic group, I was surprised—and baffled. However, rather than answer flippantly with, "Of course, there's really an afterlife," I paused; the question deserved an answer from the spirits' perspective.

As I glanced around at the people sitting before me, their loved ones in spirit stood beside them in solidarity. This is how they inspired me to answer: "As the spirits see it, there really isn't an afterlife; there is simply . . . *life*."

I went on to say:

> Maybe death isn't quite the gulf between lives that we've assumed. Maybe it is time to let go of the idea that we live one life on Earth and then, once we die, a different one lived apart from all we enjoy and the people we love. Maybe it is time to let go of the idea that death is the great separator and accept that there is continued connection between people in bodies and people in spirit. And if that's indeed the case, how might it change how we live now?

That was my answer to the cruise audience. Now, as I write this book and think about the question again, I have more I would like to say on the topic—and so do the spirits.

Many of us have grown up with the idea that there is a life beyond the physical one we're living now. The life after this one—and the location in which it is lived—is called many names: heaven, the hereafter, the Summerland, the great beyond, and nirvana, to name a few. (Interestingly, Pew Research Center states from a 2014 study that seven in ten Americans, or about 72 percent, believed in heaven.[1])

During my tenure as a medium, I've observed that as more people identify as "spiritual" rather than "religious," the afterlife has become the catchall term for whatever comes after death. It is sometimes easy to forget that not everyone agrees that there is an afterlife; and even if they do agree that there is an afterlife, they may disagree on what it is like. (A recent study by psychologists at the University of Kentucky suggests that as many as 26 percent of Americans may be atheists, not believing in a god (or gods) or a life of spirit after the physical life.[2])

I, on the other hand, had encounters with spirits at a young age, so I didn't doubt a life after this one. Being intensely curious about the nature of that "spirit life" is one of the reasons I devote my time to listening to and connecting with spirits. Maybe you share my curiosity and that is one of the reasons why you, too, are pursuing a spiritual path. Or maybe the loss of someone you love is a motivation for exploring the question, "What's next?"

As a medium, my work is grounded in interactions with spirits who provide specific and verifiable information, which I (and sometimes even the sitters) don't know or couldn't easily find out. Each and every time I communicate with spirits, the evidence supports the survival of the soul. (This book and the case studies presented are a testament to that evidence.)

Those who have died and lived to tell about it also provide evidence of an afterlife! Near-death experiencers (NDEers) share their stories with one another and publicly at chapter meetings of the International Association of Near-Death Studies (IANDS). It has been my privilege to speak to a number of these groups and share what spirits have told me about the afterlife. NDEers provide surprisingly consistent TripAdvisor-type reports of their visits to the afterlife—what they've seen and heard. In fact, many people who have died and been sent back to this world express disappointment, dismay, or anger at having to return to the body. Apparently, the afterlife gets a five-star rating. And Earth? Well, maybe one and a half stars, with much room for improvement.

I've received descriptions of the afterlife directly from spirits, which, although similar in many ways, are also surprising in their differences. For example, at a gallery-style event, I shared messages from a father in spirit who was playing cards with his buddies in spirit, a young man in spirit who announced his arrival by riding up the aisle on a motorcycle, a husband in spirit who shared his love of fishing, and a mother in spirit who reported flying on the wings of angels at the time of her death. From these descriptions, we might infer that the afterlife is part casino, part racetrack, and part deep-sea fishing adventure, with a celestial Uber service on call!

After a lifetime of meeting with spirits, I've come to understand that the afterlife is far more expansive and exquisite than our brains can grasp. Each day, I learn a little bit more, which propels me to learn even more. The task, seemingly never ending, may continue well into my own afterlife.

> *For more details on the afterlife, read the next Q&A (number 2):*
> *"Do spirits tell you what the afterlife is like?"*

4

2. Do spirits tell you what the afterlife is like?

It only makes sense to want all the details of an inevitable travel destination; but details of life in the afterlife vary, depending on the experience of the spirit with whom I'm speaking. For example, during a phone session the other day, a mother in spirit changed her outfit about six times, including shoes and handbags. Lest we think the afterlife is like New York Fashion Week, the daughter who was on the other end of the phone confirmed that her mother was known for her outstanding wardrobe.

This spirit version of *Wear This, Not That* demonstrates that we remember who we are in the afterlife. Although there is no need for clothing (because spirits don't have physical bodies), spirits can project visions of themselves so that a medium with heightened senses can see what they want to show. This show-and-tell practice that I've shared with spirits throughout the years has provided some significant indications as to what the afterlife is like.

In the afterlife, all physical limitations end.

Now, that might seem to be an obvious statement, given that spirits don't have bodies like we do. However, take a moment to consider what this really means: the physical body, which may have defined a person on the Earth plane, no longer exists in the afterlife. For example, as a medium, I have heard the voices of spirits who were mute when they lived on Earth. I've communicated with spirits who, on Earth, had lost their sight yet in the afterlife could describe in detail what their best friend looked like. I've spoken with a grandmother who suffered with Alzheimer's before she died and, from the afterlife, told her granddaughter with delight, "I've got all my marbles now!" A young man in spirit who had been paralyzed in an accident on Earth ran around my office, demonstrating to his parents that he was no longer confined to a wheelchair. I've seen the joy in a mother's face as her daughter in spirit shared that the emotional ups and downs of her life no longer plagued her.

In the afterlife, *all* physical limitations end.

In the afterlife, all that is lost is restored.

Yes, it's true that when we die, we will be with the people we loved on the Earth plane and continue those relationships; but spirits have shown me that restoration in the afterlife includes much more. Children are united with parents they may have *never* met on the Earth plane due to death, adoption, or a myriad other reasons. Broken promises of a father lost in his own addiction are mended from the afterlife. In other words, all the yearnings of the heart that we may have had and lost, or may have never even known—yearnings for love, connection, and wholeness—are ultimately restored or realized.

In the afterlife, thought is creation.

Imagine living in a world where every thought creates reality. When spirits share with me what the afterlife is like, that is the kind of world they describe. Spirits can play, build, and communicate instantly with thought. Thinking isn't planning; thinking is doing.

This instant reality of spirits may be difficult to comprehend. When I told a mother that her son in spirit thanked her for the memorial garden, she was confused: "I've been thinking about planting one but haven't had the energy to actually do it," she replied. I explained to her that her son had "heard" her thoughts and seen her vision, which made the memorial a reality to him. This doesn't mean, however, that spirits are hanging around reading our minds; when we think about someone in spirit, it is as though we send him or her a text with a picture of or a link to our thoughts.

Anyone who has tried to build a career or a dream home knows that there are many steps (and often many years) between the imagining and realization of a life dream. But in the afterlife, thought *is* creation—there is no lag time between it and the result.

In the afterlife, all that is and ever was exists in the eternal present moment.

This, perhaps, is the most difficult concept to grasp when thinking about the afterlife. There is no past, no present, and no future—at least not as we know it. And there are definitely no clocks or watches to keep track of time. For the medium, this presents a few challenges: First, spirits may choose to appear as they were at any point during their lives on Earth. Also, when spirits share information about happenings on Earth, it isn't always clear that they are speaking about something that has happened, is happening, or will happen. Fortunately, spirits know to include a date or other indication of where an event falls on our earthly timeline. In the afterlife, all that is and ever was exists in the present moment. Spirits live and communicate in the present tense.

When we hear the phrase "heaven on earth," it is typically said in reference to a place or an experience that takes us beyond the everyday—something blissful, extraordinary. Well, I think that one of the reasons spirits speak with me is so that I can convey the ways in which we can make "heaven on earth" an everyday experience.

In thinking about how this could be, consider for a moment which ideas about personal physical limitations could be let go. Stories about people who have overcome great odds or physical disabilities to succeed at sports or in the arts inspire us for that very reason. Just as we thrill for the competitors in the Special Olympics or on *America's Got Talent*, loved ones in spirit encourage us to step beyond any limitations we think we may have, either physically or due to other life circumstances.

These circumstances may include the painful loss of loved ones, of a home from a collapsed economy, of a job due to downsizing, of a country due to the ravages of war. Spirits speak of the possibility of restoration, not just in the afterlife but here.

For example, I was enjoying a session with a woman in her early fifties and her parents in spirit when the oddest thing happened. Her father held up a sign that said, "It's a boy!" and her mother held up a sign that said, "It's a girl!" When I shared this display with their daughter, she laughed and told me that she was wondering if her parents knew about her children. As was later revealed, their daughter had wanted children more than anything in the world, but infertility dashed her dreams. After both her parents passed, she adopted two beautiful children—a girl and a boy. Her hope was restored, and the children found a mother to love and care for them.

If you want to live like the spirits while still inhabiting a physical body, recognizing that thought is creative is one of the simplest yet (not always easiest) ways. Each thought either limits possibilities or allows us to embrace all that is available to us; so, wanting a change in life is directly related to changing thoughts. Take time to listen to what you're saying to yourself because the spirits and the Universe are listening too. If you think that the cards are stacked against you or that you always get the short end of the stick, everything in life will support that belief, making it reality.

And finally, remember that the only place to meet spirits is in the present moment. They're not hanging out somewhere in the past, nor do we need to chase them into the future. They are here *right now*. All that you are and all that they are exists in this place and in this eternal, present moment. Here. And. Now.

3. Is there a difference between a ghost and a spirit?

The words *ghost* and *spirit* are often used interchangeably. The phrase "give up the ghost," which may have originated in the Bible, has been used historically to refer to the moment of death. It's not surprising, therefore, that "giving up the ghost" has extended its meaning to indicate that anyone who dies *is* a ghost.

I, however, differentiate between ghosts and spirits, and made that distinction early in my life: spirits were people I knew and loved, like my grandfather, while ghosts were strangers marching up the stairs to my room at night. Being a child, this wasn't a distinction based on knowledge and experience but, rather, simple instinct—an intuitive "stranger danger" designation. Even at a young age, I sensed that there were spirits who were loving and caring toward me, and there were others who simply went about their business; if these others noticed me, however, they didn't seem nice or friendly. Later on, to make sense of all this, I studied everything I could find about ghosts and spirits.

During my teens, I joined the Rosicrucian Order (a commu-
nity of mystics who study and practice esoteric wisdom) and read
books—many by American author and parapsychologist Hans
Holzer—hoping to understand the intersection of the living with
the dead. As a result, in my twenties, my interaction with the world
of the paranormal had a ghost-busting emphasis. For example, in
the early 1990s, I met a young couple with a perplexing ghost problem. Each time they had sex in their bedroom, they were startled by
the appearance of an old man (whom they referred to as a ghost). The
ghost was quite put out by these strangers in his bedroom, and made
it known by his sudden and indiscreet presence. He wanted to know:
"Why are these people in my house?"

The struggle over ownership of a piece of property is one of the
indicators that an entity is a ghost rather than a spirit. The unwilling-
ness to let go of a physical location demonstrates that a ghost remains
attached to physical life. A spirit, on the other hand, may make an
appearance in a house in which they lived, but the purpose is to make
connection with a loved one still living there.

Sometimes a ghost doesn't know he or she is dead, or is unwilling
to acknowledge it. I've seen this most often in circumstances when
dying is sudden and the body and surroundings are destroyed as well.
Though this is traumatic to imagine, don't worry; in these cases, there
are always "first responders" in spirit who can help sudden spirits
adjust to life without a body.

Also, a ghost may want to air a grievance of one sort or another.
It might be easy to think of it this way: a ghost is a spirit with a bad
attitude. And boy, I've met a few. During ghostly encounters, I have
even been physically harmed, though not in any lasting way. My
hair has been pulled, I've been tripped in a stairwell, and I've been
pushed and prodded by ghosts trying to get my attention. After one
of these ugly encounters, I decided this workplace harassment wasn't
worth the trouble and retired from the ghost-busting business.

Fortunately, I discovered that the frequency (the vibrational rate) of connection could be accessed and set by using meditation. Since I desired to use the vibration of love to bring healing to the world through my work, it was essential to align with spirits who shared the same frequency of love.

I didn't simply stumble upon the frequency of love but, rather, remembered it from my years of singing in church. My mother raised me as a church musician, always in choir. Eventually, I traveled with a music ministry, supporting physical and spiritual healing at the frequency of love. It is at this frequency that I now meet with spirits. At this frequency, there is no more negative physical contact and there are no more grievances to air; and the work relationship is one of mutual respect. Spirits at this frequency are kind, and their messages are hopeful and helpful. Communicating with these loving spirits is what gets me out of bed in the morning.

That doesn't mean that I don't still bump into bad-tempered ghosts now and again. Several years ago, I visited the old mining town of Jerome, Arizona, with a friend who is also a medium. What we thought was going to be a lovely afternoon enjoying history, boutiques, and artisanal cuisine became fraught with pushy ghosts instead—literally. As we walked through the hilly town, I could feel pressure against my back. At the moment I was about to fall over, my friend asked, "Do you feel a group behind us—pushing us along? Should we find out what they want?"

"Yes, I feel them," I replied, "and no, let's not stop and chat with a ghost gang. Keep moving!"

We settled into a lovely restaurant, and after ordering lavender lemonade, I noticed my friend's eyes grow alarmingly wide.

"There's a man's face over your shoulder—he's green!" she said, immediately calling to mind Nickelodeon slime.

With that, I had the sense of a knife being plunged into my left side. Although it wasn't painful, there was a feeling of penetration. A man's voice in my ear started to tell a story of betrayal and death in an old mining town. There was no ignoring him, so I let him know that he was being heard. I also asked protective spirits to help guide this man to love and healing—and away from me.

My friend and I changed tables and finished our lemonade. Later that day, we saw a sign that proudly proclaimed: "Jerome, the most haunted town in America." Well, of course—if you advertise this slogan, every disgruntled ghost is going to take up residence! And why might this be? The sign and collective desire of visitors to see ghosts declares the intention (and sets the frequency) for manifestation. The collective energy of that intention is the equivalent of an email blast inviting ghosts from far and wide!

During a recent phone session, I spoke with a young woman who was making a ghost feel very much at home. She had purchased a house (her first) and was doing everything possible to please a ghost who had previously lived and died there. "He likes it when I turn on the lights at five in the afternoon," she told me. "And he lets me know when he's unhappy—he bangs on the walls."

"Is he paying rent?" I asked her.

She laughed, even though I wasn't trying to be funny.

Danielle had hoped to get a message from her couch-surfing ghost, but instead, we connected with an unexpected—and unwanted— spirit: her grandfather Kurt. At first, Danielle was resistant to hearing from this grandfather, and I soon learned why: I smelled alcohol from him and felt great remorse. Kurt projected a vision of a clock into my mind, and I heard it chime five times.

When I shared this with Danielle, she wept and then told me why she was crying. Her mother, following a brutal divorce, took Danielle to live with her grandfather. She was alone with Kurt after school each day, and it was his habit to drink heavily in the afternoons. As he became drunk, he also became verbally abusive. At 5:00 PM each day, he ordered her to turn the lights on to welcome her mother home. If she didn't move fast enough, he would bang books on a table or throw things at her. As Danielle's story ended with a sigh, I was overcome with remorse once again and heard, "So sorry."

Following her grandfather's apology, Danielle reconsidered her willingness to host a curmudgeon ghost who interfered with her life when he didn't get his way. She was also willing to redefine her idea of "home." She declared, "I want my new home to be my safe place and mine, only mine." So, although it was a ghost that initially brought Danielle to me, it was the spirit of a remorseful grandfather, willing to own his actions, who led her to a peaceful home.

Before our session ended, I suggested to Danielle that she secure a referral for a practitioner who specializes in clearing the energy of homes in which unwanted guests have taken up residence. Mediums like Mary Ann Winkowski, whose work inspired the TV show *Ghost Whisperer*, specialize in helping ghosts move on. It is important to note that no ghost has to remain "stuck," and no one has to continually suffer pain after death, whether emotional or physical. The pathway to love and light is always clear, and helpful mediums and spirits can lead the way. In essence, a ghost *can* become a spirit!

After Danielle and I said goodbye, I had to sit quietly for some time. The parallels between Danielle's childhood and her current experience with a demanding house ghost stunned even me. I could see that Danielle's childhood fear and abuse from her grandfather made it easier for her to "accept" an abusive ghost. By forgiving and healing the past, she now had the courage to stand up for herself and face her present situation. Once again, I was reminded of the potent power of working at the frequency of love.

In conclusion, Danielle's story also illustrates some of the differences I've noticed between ghosts and spirits. They are:

* Ghosts are attached to places on Earth; spirits remain connected to loved ones.

* Ghosts can be demanding; spirits are respectful.

* Ghosts hang on to grievances and anger; spirits take responsibility for their actions.

* Ghosts are resistant to change; spirits are willing to share their own transformation and encourage healing in others.

* Ghosts are energized by fear; spirits are powered by love.

> For more on "first responders" in spirit, read Q&A number 59,
> "Are spirits aware of disasters, including ecological ones?"
> in chapter 9, "The Big Questions."

4. So, what's a medium, anyway?

A medium is a person who receives verifiable information from spirits and conveys messages to people in the physical world. The information is evidence that life continues beyond death, and the messages provide comfort following the loss of a loved one. To better understand this definition, it may help to differentiate a medium from a psychic and a channeler, which people often assume are synonymous.

What makes a psychic, a medium, and a channeler different isn't how each receives information but, rather, the *source* from which it is received. A psychic interprets *energy* around people, places, and things on Earth. This information is helpful for getting a "take" on current situations and future possibilities, including if Mr. Right is about to enter your life. A channeler, on the other hand, receives *messages* from one or more spirit entities (some of whom may never have lived on Earth). These spirits are dedicated to helping the masses expand consciousness and spiritual awareness. Messages through a channeler are helpful for shifting limiting beliefs toward a broader understanding of life.

To further illustrate the contrast between these practitioners and their work, let me share an example from my own life:

One lovely spring day, I was browsing in a metaphysical bookstore when I saw a notice that a psychic was on call and available for walk-ins. At the time, I was grappling (or perhaps I should say *hoping*) that a relationship I was in would progress to marriage. When I sat down with the psychic, who used tarot cards as a tool to interpret energy, he asked me to hold the cards while concentrating on my question. After he laid out the cards in a spread (an arrangement which indicates past, present, and future influences), he looked up at me somewhat startled and said, "There's death all around you." I assured him that I understood the reference. He asked me to voice my question, which I did. After a few more exclamations about the dead and dying (which I was convinced had nothing to do with my dating question), he started to describe the man I loved. When I pressed him about whether the relationship would be successful and long lasting, he replied, "Eighty-five percent positive; but you travel a lot for work, yes?" I replied in the affirmative, and he ended with "Fifteen percent trouble with the relationship because of travel." I walked away somewhat buoyed. After all, what's 15 percent? A mere glitch, perhaps.

Not long after that, I was given a gift of a psychic reading by a friend. I set up the appointment and drove deep into the San Fernando Valley. As soon as I sat down, the female psychic said, "You have a man in spirit with you—I hear the name 'John Gibson.' But I'm not a medium, you understand. I'm a psychic."

Well, it was now *my* turn to be puzzled and startled. John Gibson is the name of my grandfather (his first and middle names)—and she saw him with me! As the reading continued, the "psychic" said, "There is a lady in spirit who calls you 'Holly Dolly.' But I'm not a medium, you understand. I'm a psychic."

What? "Holly Dolly" was my grandmother's favorite nickname for me!

The messages continued with the "I'm not a medium" disclaimer inserted far too often. It was clear to me that this lovely psychic was a medium who was either confused about her talent for connecting to spirits or afraid to admit it for some reason! My jaw nearly dropped to the floor when she said this: "The John spirit knows about the man you love. He asks you if the man you love loves your work enough to support you in it." Well, I hadn't really considered whether my boyfriend loved my work; I thought that if he loved me, that would be enough.

Within the same week, I attended a channeling event. The channeler gave a brief talk and description of how she worked: while in a trance state, she answered questions in the manner and with the wisdom of a spirit group who call themselves "Vashti." The spirit group was described by the channeler as a consortium of spirits who hadn't lived on Earth but had chosen her as the one to share their higher understanding of spiritual principles. I, of course, asked about my relationship (what else?). Here is part of the answer: "You who speak of love and share love with all, be reminded that love for yourself, without condition, is of high value as well."

I didn't have time to reflect on what the channeler said because I was leaving for New York early the next morning. Once settled into my hotel, I called my boyfriend who, without preamble, said, "Our relationship isn't what I want it to be. You're devoted to your work and you travel too much. Maybe if you moved to San Diego and settled down, we would have a chance."

"I can't do that," I replied, knowing that to scale-down travel would also mean limiting the reach of my work. And with that, the relationship ended.

My first thought was, *That darn 15 percent!* However, after I cried (which I did so enthusiastically that my neighbor in the next room called the front desk!), I sat and reflected. Each of the practitioners—the psychic, the medium, and the channeler—provided guidance that was helpful. The psychic made the link between the potential problems with the relationship and my work. The medium, who thought she was a psychic, provided evidence that my beloved grandfather and grandmother were with me. My grandfather raised the very question I had neglected to ask myself. And the channeler, although prompted by my question, gave an answer that is of value to many people whose mission is to help others. (By the way, that message from Vashti helped me to direct my energy toward self-care following the breakup.)

Not only were all three readings helpful in preparing me for moving through the aftermath of relationship disappointment, they also reoriented my attitude toward a romantic relationship. From that point on, I knew that intimacy must include an appreciation for my work as a medium.

You may think it strange that a medium would seek out the services of a psychic, a medium, and a channeler; but being a medium doesn't mean that you don't need any help! Although I know that my loved ones are with me and I am guided, my connection to spirits is a work of service to others. And therefore, when I'm seeking an answer for my own life questions, I, just like you, seek the counsel and support of psychics, mediums, and channelers. Lucky for me, many of the finest and best are my dearest friends.

As was made evident by the psychic in my story, who couldn't admit to being a medium, there is considerable confusion, even among practitioners themselves, about the differences between a psychic, a medium, and a channeler. The reason for this is that all these practitioners receive and interpret information in similar ways, and will blend information from earthly and nonearthly sources.

Psychics, mediums, and channelers receive information via energy centers in the body called chakras. *Chakra* is a Sanskrit word that translates to "wheel." Some disciplines suggest that there are many of these wheels of energy in the human body through which a person's life force intersects with the physical and nonphysical (consciousness). Psychics, mediums, and channelers tend to work primarily with seven of these wheels of energy, which align along the spine from just below the coccyx (the root chakra) to the center of the top of the head (the crown chakra). Chakras are associated with a heightened sense of sight, smell, taste, hearing, and feeling.

These heightened senses are referred to as the "clairs." *Clairvoyance*, *clairaudience*, *clairaliance*, *clairsentience*, and *clairgustance*—French terms meaning clear seeing, clear hearing, clear smelling, clear feeling, and clear tasting. Psychics, mediums, and channelers can all be clairvoyant. For instance, they can receive information at the sixth energy center in their bodies, known as the third eye (positioned in the middle of the forehead), which corresponds with the ability to see energy, symbols, and spirits. This is true for all the other clairs and their corresponding chakras as well.

When connecting with spirits as a medium, it's an interactive experience. Spirits move during communication, and there may be more than one visiting at a time. This action-packed presence of the spirits is helpful, especially at large events, when a blur or moving figure will catch my eye. Almost always, that movement directs my attention to where the spirits want me to begin providing messages. (It is also important to note that some practitioners refer to themselves as "psychic mediums." This simply means that information provided is from a blending of sources—the energy around people, places, and things on Earth as well as spirits.)

Psychics, mediums, and channelers aren't the only ones who use energy centers for "reading" the landscape of life or connecting with spirits. Everyone does! Intuition or gut feeling is not only your personal protection system but also a guide on your spiritual journey. (An excellent book on the subject is Sara Wiseman's *The Intuitive Path*.)

The sense that a loved one in spirit is with you may be the result of your energy centers recognizing a familiar personality. Flashes of insight and a growing sense of being connected to all may be a soul-awakening moment that has the potential to become an awakened life. And ultimately, the more "in tune" we become to the energy around us and to the spirits who love us, the more we can be of service to one another.

5. What is mediumship for?

When I received a call that someone I loved very much had died suddenly, I heard a crack within my chest, fell to the floor, and thought, *I just heard my heart break.*

That heartbreak brought tremendous life changes, as loss and grief often do. I felt vulnerable and broken in every way. "How can I go on?" I asked, often crying myself to sleep. Being a medium didn't inoculate me from grief. So, if mediumship doesn't prevent suffering, even for a medium, what purpose and value does it have?

The simple answer is this: mediumship (or "spirit communication," as it is also called) provides a pathway toward healing of all kinds.

When my heart broke, I couldn't find my way out of the pain. It wasn't until friends of mine, also mediums, made me (yes, *made me*) meet with them as a group that I experienced the healing power of mediumship firsthand. As we gathered together in a candlelit living room, each medium friend, in turn, provided a message from the person I loved. When a large candle on the table burned to a nub in a minute (literally!), we all laughed. The one I loved, who was a charismatic actor, always had to be the brightest presence in any room. No candle could possibly be competition! It was in shared laughter and joy that I took the first step down the pathway toward healing.

Here are some of the ways mediumship can be helpful to the healing process:

Mediumship provides a pathway toward healing by presenting evidence.

The information that a medium receives from spirits may include names, cause of death, relationship to the sitter, career, personality type, favorite hobbies and the like. The more personal and specific the evidence, the more confident a sitter can be that a loved one has survived death and the medium is communicating with that spirit.

Mediumship provides a pathway toward healing by offering closure.

Saying what needs to be said and hearing what needs to be heard— these are two gifts mediumship offers to the bereaved on Earth. A woman who attended a gallery-style event experienced this kind of healing and posted this message to my Facebook page:

Hearing from my ex-husband who passed means I can move forward with no more whys, what ifs, guilt, and resentment. I feel renewed and able to move on, with great things to come on my journey in life.[3]

Please note that "moving on" in the context of mediumship doesn't mean that we leave behind loved ones in spirit. What it does mean is that the pain of unfinished business is left behind, making peace possible, even with the most difficult of situations.

> **Mediumship provides a pathway toward healing on multiple levels—the physical, the emotional, and the spiritual.**

Spiritualist churches often hold healing services, where trained healers act as conduits of energy between spirits and sitters. (Spiritualist churches, as part of the movement known as Spiritualism, which began in the mid-1800s, are based on the belief that spirits do exist and interact with the living.) Whenever I attend services at a Spiritualist church, I ask for healing too, sometimes receiving bursts of energy that help sustain my work as a medium. Even if there isn't a Spiritualist church in your area, the power of prayer is still available to you. Many churches, including Spiritualist churches, place those in need on a prayer list. Prayer requests can be made online as well at unity.org/prayer, for example. The supportive healing energy of prayer helped me immensely as I was recovering from a broken ankle, for example. The doctor was surprised, maybe more than I was, that the break healed perfectly and in less time than expected.

Because mediumship falls into the category of the "healing arts," it shouldn't be surprising that the number of mediums who identify as "medical mediums" is on the rise. With the historical link between mediumship and (spiritual, emotional, and physical) healing established by spiritualists and American psychic Edgar Cayce (known as the "sleeping prophet"), who founded the Association for Research and Enlightenment (ARE) in 1931, this next wave of popular mediumship makes sense.

Yes, mediumship is a pathway toward healing. But in an even broader sense, mediumship is a cooperative, ongoing experiment for mediums, spirits, and sitters, reminding us that we all are in this thing called life, together. At its essence, mediumship offers healing to humanity by comforting one broken heart at a time, even the broken heart of a medium.

2

On Being a Medium

6. Do psychic and mediumship abilities run in families?

As far as I know, no DNA markers for psychic ability have been identified. However, despite the lack of irrefutable proof that these abilities run in families, personal experiences and observations support that where there is one psychic in a family, there are often more.

The best place to start, perhaps, is with my own family. My mother used to jokingly say, "I have eyes in the back of my head." And she did! One afternoon, I got home from school before she arrived. When she called to check on me, her first words were, "Stop eating my Mallomars." This chocolate-covered-marshmallow-on-a-graham-cracker treat was my mom's favorite—and only available during certain months of the year. My hand had been in the cookie jar at the moment she called. My mother's prescience freaked me out! So, whenever she said, "Mark my words," I did. My mother always knew what the next best step would be in my schooling, my musical education, and my career. Her astute intuition and assessment of people's behaviors was uncanny, and her confidence was utterly otherworldly.

But my mother isn't the only one with these abilities. My sister, Wendy, is also a sensitive who communicates with spirits. And my auntie Sue, sensitive to spirits herself, moved deeper into that world following the death of my cousin, Tommy. Auntie Sue not only sensed when Tommy was with her during the day but also visited with him in dreams at night.

Not only does psychic and spirit sensitivity run in my family but creativity does as well. My mother was an amazing "by ear" piano player; and I, too, am a pianist, going to conservatory and later traveling with singing groups during my early teen years. My mother's grandfather was a writer, and I recently came across a handwritten book of poetry by my mother's aunt Day. On my dad's side, Aunt Ellen, his sister, wrote a book of poetry, which was published shortly before her death and distributed at her funeral. Not to be left out, my father has always been termed "dramatic" by my mother, his primary audience, most usually on matters pertaining to money.

Generally speaking, I have found it to be true that when spirit sensitivity runs in families, it is often accompanied by a natural creativity, musical or otherwise. My extensive work with creative professionals in the entertainment industry underscores the link between creativity and psychic and spirit sensitivity. Nearly all of the actors, writers, and musicians with whom I've worked acknowledge that, in their creativity, they connect with someone or something beyond themselves.

People who don't consider themselves a creative type may say something like "you have an amazing gift" to a medium in much the same way they would to a singer. However, using "gift" in terms of psychic and mediumship ability is inaccurate. Why is that? Well, first of all, I considered sensitivity to spirits much more a curse than a gift in my early years. And, more important, mediumship is a talent rather than a gift. Like other talents—for instance, singing or dancing—it's something you're born to do. However, expertise in that talent is the result of learning and practice. So when someone says, "I'm a natural-born medium," that may indeed be true, but it is only half the story. Mediums are both born and made. This is why I teach mediumship—to help make it easier for others to develop their natural talent.

When I first started teaching mediumship more than two decades ago, I noticed that the incredibly sensitive people showing up to class often came from very difficult family backgrounds. Family dynamics included substance abuse, abuse of other kinds, and neglect. After meeting many such sensitives, it became clear to me, with the help of spirits, that personal healing is also a part of becoming a medium. As I tell my students, we can't bring people to a place of healing when we ourselves haven't been healed. As I met wounded sensitives, one after another, I knew that there was also a link between painful childhoods and spontaneous psychic and mediumship development. It seemed to me that psychic sensitivity was a survival instinct activated to navigate life circumstances, which were often unsteady, unfathomable, and unbearable.

There is another point I'd like to make: if psychic and mediumship ability is a talent, then it doesn't follow that a medium is a spiritually superior human being. Just because someone is a great psychic or a great medium doesn't mean that he or she is a great spiritual leader or guru. Yes, I understand that the talent and general gorgeousness of Bruno Mars and Adele make them deserving of devotion, but their talent doesn't make them the spiritual leaders of a generation. So, it is important not to imbue psychics and mediums with undue reverence either!

A note to parents of children with psychic or mediumship abilities or both

When I was young, it wasn't cool—actually, it wasn't even *acceptable*— to be a medium. Seeing spirits meant that you were crazy, and there was more than one person who thought that to be true of me. As a result, I learned to conceal my ability to see spirits. My parents didn't encourage spirit communication, but they were very kind in helping to soothe my nighttime fear and anxiety, the result of ghosts invading my space. One of their tricks was to keep the lights on until after I had fallen asleep—a simple yet welcome comfort.

Fortunately, times have changed a great deal since my childhood; and being highly sensitive is no longer something to hide but, rather, to accept. These days, young parents contact me because they want to support the natural sensitivity their children exhibit. What I suggest is that they talk with their children in a matter-of-fact way about what their children are experiencing. Rather than working with children directly, I find that it's more effective to teach and provide parents with a working knowledge of spirit communication. I've made this choice because the bodies of children are growing, and their energy centers grow and develop along with their bodies. Energy work can be intense, but parents can help to lay the groundwork for the future development of their children. In my workshops, parents learn how to do simple and fun exercises and meditations for grounding and protection. Kids have great imaginations, so the stories that accompany guided meditations can be both fun and effective.

One of the reasons I have a heart for this work is because I didn't have a childhood mentor who could have demystified something that I felt was happening *to* me—more of an affliction than something that could be of benefit. Fortunately, in my twenties, I connected with influential mediums and sat in circles for mediumship development. By the time I stepped into working as a medium, I had spent decades studying books on the subject and practicing spirit communication with other talented mediums.

Many of the difficulties faced by mediums of earlier times are falling away with the more widespread acceptance of spirit communication. This is an exciting time to be a psychic, medium, or channeler; it can even be an accepted career! In my day, psychic sensitivity wasn't tested on the SATs, but who knows? Maybe someday, it will be!

7. Do all spirits communicate with mediums in the same way?

Unfortunately, no. But it would make it so much easier for mediums if they did!

The spirits' desire to communicate specific information as evidence that they have survived death is important to them, but this evidence doesn't always come to the medium in ways that are expected or preferred. In some cases, spirits can provide so much information that it is almost overwhelming—as the following example demonstrates:

> "A male in spirit is standing next to you; he's holding up a guitar."
>
> "Yes!" the female sitter exclaimed and started to cry.
>
> "He looks great in a pair of jeans," I added.
>
> "Yes!" she exclaimed in response.
>
> "I'm hearing the *vroom-vroom* of a motorcycle."
>
> "Yes!" she shouted with even more tears.
>
> "Accidental drug overdose," I reported.
>
> "Yes, oh yes . . ." she whispered with a sob.

This dramatic call and response between the spirit and sitter continued for some time. With each piece of information, the spirit revealed a well-rounded picture of himself and his relationship to the beautiful young woman sitting before me.

The calling out of identifying characteristics isn't the norm but is representative of the creative and dramatic manner in which this particular spirit had lived. Personally, I prefer that spirits identify themselves in an orderly way; and my agreements with the spirit world reflect that. These agreements, developed over time and with much trial and error, are essentially a "rulebook of etiquette" for interacting with spirits. Agreements streamline communication and provide shorthand for understanding how spirits are related to the sitter and to one another. Just as there is a protocol for introducing people to one another at a business meeting or a party, a similar protocol can be applied to spirit introductions.

Consider a business meeting, where it's common to find people who sit around a conference table in accordance with their status within the company and their relationship to their coworkers. Similarly, when I start a meeting with spirits, each spirit stands in relation to the sitter, indicating to me whether that spirit is a father, a mother, a sister, or a close friend. As I look at the sitter, spirits to their left tend to be from the mother's family, and spirits on the right are from the father's. So, when I see a spirit standing close to a sitter on the right, that spirit is either a father or a father figure (perhaps a stepfather or a grandfather who served as a father). This does not mean that spirits live life in the afterlife like guests at a wedding, divided into the bride's or the groom's side at the church; it is simply a construct I use to make communication easier. Additionally, I know that the closer a spirit stands to the sitter, the closer the relationship they share—the distance between a spirit and the sitter exemplifies distance in the relationship. Every medium develops his or her personal way of organizing sessions, and mine certainly isn't the only way!

You may wonder, *How do spirits know where to stand?* and the answer is simple: I have spirit guides who work with me. I request the help of these guides during a blessing and ask out loud before the start of each session or event. Although I don't see these guides during sessions (that would be way too confusing!), I can imagine them saying to their fellow spirits, "Stand here, and she'll know you're a father," or "Move over there, so she'll know that you were absent from your daughter's life."

That said, despite all this planning, I am committed to presenting spirits as they choose, following their lead even if it is unexpected or uncomfortable for me. Consequently, this commitment and trust in my agreements with spirits have allowed me to be confident in connections even when relationships don't fall in line with the expected.

In addition to visual cues, such as sitter location, spirits will use my clairsentience (clear feeling) to provide information regarding their relationship to the sitter. For example, at an event, a man in spirit gave me a feeling of "husband" as he stood next to a woman sitter in the audience. "No, I don't have a husband who has passed," she announced. The audience was audibly disappointed that I had gotten it wrong. Refusing to move on, the spirit continued to give me the feeling of "husband." Finally, after he gave me the name "Jorge," the sitter confessed. "Jorge was my boyfriend for twenty-two years," she admitted, "but we never got married. It is one of my greatest regrets." Apparently, Jorge saw himself as a husband, and by identifying as such, was offering healing for a regret. There was a collective "Awwww" from the audience, medium included.

During a private session, a spirit used my clairaudience (heightened sense of clear hearing) to announce her presence in a memorable manner. "Your mother, Clarice, is here," I shared with a stylish woman in her late thirties.

She laughed uproariously until tears rolled down her cheeks. (I didn't see the humor in this.) "My mom's favorite movie was *Silence of the Lambs*, and she was a huge Jodie Foster fan," the sitter explained. "As a family joke, we started calling her 'Clarice.'"

Speaking of movies, I live in Los Angeles, and many of my clients are in the entertainment industry. Therefore, it shouldn't be surprising that I've also spoken with the rich and famous in spirit. I bring this up not to impress you with my connections with spirit celebrities (who shun selfies, by the way), but to make this point: spirits who were famous on Earth almost always avoid giving me a glimpse of their iconic selves. This was underscored at a spirit circle when a father in spirit took charge of the room.

The spirit spoke about his dying experience, especially the final three days. He provided specific information about his relationship to a few women in the circle, during which other spirits joined him for the visit. His big personality and humor had all of us in the room laughing, accompanying spirits included. However, when his daughter asked, "Is he showing you an Emmy?" I was at a loss. I know what an Emmy looks like; and it would have been easy for the spirit to impress that image upon my mind, but he hadn't. It seemed that he was much more interested in talking about his family and his dog (who was there with him in spirit too). After the messages from her father were completed, this daughter told me who her famous father (actually, stepfather) was in this life.

So why wouldn't a spirit identify himself or herself by Emmy, Tony, or Oscar? The answer is simple: it is more important to spirits that they reestablish a relationship with those they love on Earth rather than enlisting another fan—namely me, the medium. In all honesty, it might be difficult for anyone, including an ethical medium, to set aside what he or she might assume is true about a famous person. However, when a spirit communicates from the heart with specific information that only those closest would know, it is the best validation for those who grieve for them. After all, spirit communication isn't an awards show. And during a session, the actor, producer, or director *never* forgets to thank his or her family!

The way in which spirits make themselves known to me has everything to do with how they want to be remembered by the people they love. The essence of the relationship is more important than the legalities of it. This allows for a boyfriend to step into the role of a husband, a mother to cause laughter by taking on a screen character, and a famous person to remain anonymous. Love is not only the constant of communication but also the very reason for it.

> For more on spirit guides, read Q&A number 36, "What is the difference between guides and angels?" and Q&A number 37, "How can I meet my spirit guide?" in chapter 5, "Afterlife Relationships."

8. Can mediums communicate with spirits who speak a different language?

Before the days of Google Translate, I heard a crash outside my Hollywood, California, apartment late one afternoon. When I ran out the door to see what had happened, two people were getting out of two cars with dented fenders. They commenced shouting at each other in different languages, neither of which I could understand, then they turned to me in a perfectly choreographed way, as though I were the solution to their language problem. I shrugged, which they understood, and called the police.

Fortunately, as a medium, I don't have to resort to shrugging when speaking with spirits. Much of the evidence spirits provide isn't language based but visual, so it doesn't need to be translated at all. For example, when I saw a spirit dressed in black with a Mohawk hairstyle and piercings everywhere, it didn't matter that I didn't speak his native German. His cousin, who had come to a spirit circle, knew exactly who he was when I gave her a description.

Spirits provide information in a variety of ways, including symbols, feelings, and visions. This method of communication is effective in much the same way as internationally standardized signs are helpful to travelers needing a restroom or a first-aid station.

I've had extensive experience speaking with spirits who didn't know English while they were living on Earth. This is mostly because I live in Los Angeles, where more than two hundred languages are spoken. In addition, my first book was published in other languages and distributed worldwide, which has resulted in my speaking with spirits from countries other than the United States as well.

During sessions in which clients don't speak English, a third party—either a family member or a paid translator—helps us to understand one another. (The irony that I need a translator to speak with people on Earth yet don't need one to communicate with spirits isn't lost on me!)

Sometimes spirits choose to share languages other than English as evidence of family ancestry, in most cases. Fortunately, I have a knack for recognizing languages because I've traveled a lot in my life, have sung music in different languages, and in general, have a good ear for them. My agreement with spirits is that when I hear language coming from behind me, it represents the language of their ancestors. When I hear a language being spoken in my ear, it indicates that the spirit I'm speaking with knew and spoke that language on Earth. (Please note that this may not be the same for all mediums. We each develop a lexicon of communication with spirits.)

During one session, a beautiful young boy of about eleven, who had passed with cancer, provided information in a unique way. In my inner ear, I heard what sounded like odd bits of English—the words seemed out of order. I ignored it, but it persisted. As I listened, I realized where

I had heard speaking like this: onscreen in *Star Wars*, from Yoda! As I relayed this to the boy's mother, she gasped. "Brian *loved Star Wars*, and Yoda was his favorite character!" Once again, language can be a gateway rather than a barrier to communication. Just remembering this encounter with Yoda-ese makes me smile.

There are times when a single word in a language I don't know speaks volumes of pain and suffering. For example, in Denver, at a spirit circle gathering, a father in spirit said something that I didn't understand.

"I'm hearing what sounds like 'Do-too?' said again and again," I told a young woman sitting in the back of the room.

Her mouth dropped open. "How do you know that word?" she asked.

"I don't know the word, but that is the sound I'm hearing in my ear," I said. "What does it mean?"

This young woman explained that her father had been saying the Chinese word for "gambler" (which happens to be *dǔ tú*). She went on to say that her family had once been wealthy, but her grandfather had such a gambling addiction that all was lost. The result was that members of the family emigrated to America and other countries, and had to begin again.

Dǔ tú—one word, a world of meaning.

Emotions and physical pain don't need translation either. The feeling of love, for instance, is the same in all languages. Love expands within my chest—so much that I can barely breathe at times. If a spirit wants to provide evidence that he died of a heart attack, I may feel a sharp and sudden pain in my own heart. A popping sound in my head signals that the spirit died from damage due to a brain aneurysm.

During a session with a client named Bor, I said, "I feel as though my legs have been cut off at the knees." Bor acknowledged that his grandfather had both legs amputated from the knee down due to a farming accident. His grandfather had lived in Slovenia and didn't speak English at all, but he certainly got his point across.

Bor, who had been named after his grandfather, expressed great concern that he wouldn't be able to speak with his own grandfather in the afterlife; they have the same DNA but don't share a language. This is the case for many of us and our ancestors in spirit. For example, my ancestors are German, English, Irish, and Scottish; does this mean that I can only enjoy the company of the side of the family that speaks English?

Have no fear. In the afterlife, there is communication beyond the divisions caused by language on Earth—a universal language bridging realms. The reason I know this is that when I meet spirits from different generations and different parts of the world, there is instant communication among them. The afterlife is a world of expanded, linked, and shared consciousness of understanding. I wish that I could explain exactly how family members from different centuries, cultures, and countries communicate and remain eternally connected, but I don't know the mechanics of it. I will someday, however, as will you!

Perhaps the only thing we really need to know right now is that *all* spirits, regardless of language, can use my clairsentience (sense of feeling) to express love for those they've left behind. And that feeling of love is unmistakable; it is *never* lost in translation.

For more on communicating with spirits from past generations, read Q&A number 45, "Is it possible to communicate with our ancestors?" in chapter 6, "The Language of Spirits."

9. Have you communicated with transsexual and transgender spirits?

When I first started working as a medium, I made a commitment to communicate with all spirits who come in love. That decision made me available to speak with guides, angels, animals, and people of all genders and sexual orientations. That being said, when I made that commitment more than a quarter century ago, sexual identity wasn't the topic of discussion and means of identification that it is today. Consequently, there were fewer people who identified as transsexual or transgender communicating with me. In recent years, that has changed.

With that change, my mantra, "Give it as you get it," or providing information from spirits without interpretation, has become even more important. This was highlighted when I saw a young female in spirit standing next to a woman at a gallery event.

"This spirit feels like a daughter," I stated. The woman in the audience didn't respond to that statement. "I'm hearing the name Tom."

"My son has passed, and his name is Tom," she replied. This puzzled me because I didn't see a son in spirit but, rather, a spirit I thought was daughter. After more messages from the spirit, it became clear that the daughter in spirit I was seeing was the son, Tom, who had transitioned from male to female. Tom's mother hadn't come to terms with this transition before her daughter's sudden death. However, this loving daughter made it clear that she understood the confusion her mother felt prior to her death, and the pain of loss she was feeling now. In presenting herself as female in spirit, while additionally providing the name Tom, the daughter not only validated her gender identity but also reminded her mother that she was the child to whom her mother had given birth.

At a recent spirit circle, a female spirit appeared next to Mario, a young man in the group. The spirit had a theatrical manner and had highly arched eyebrows. When I described her as a "diva," Mario knew exactly who she was. This flamboyant, overly dramatic woman had started out life on Earth as a man, but in the early 1960s, had chosen to live as a woman. Mario's connection to her was through her best friend, with whom he had recently moved in and who had also written a book about the female spirit's life. The diva provided specific personal details (including her alcoholism and Hollywood connections) and, at one point, yelled, "Surprise!" Neither Mario nor I understood what this exclamation meant, but the session continued on.

The next person in spirit who appeared was Mario's mother. She also yelled, "Surprise!" but this time, the reference was obvious: "I was a surprise," he replied. "My mother was forty-two when she had me, and the pregnancy wasn't planned."

Just then, I got a sudden shot to the heart and the feeling that his mother hadn't accepted the fact that he is gay. When I shared that information, he confirmed that his coming out wasn't met with happiness; yet his mother went on to say, "I accept you as you are. I love you. You are my son."

While the entire group at the circle wiped their tears, the diva's big "surprise" was now clear. Not only had Mario's mother come to visit him and share her love and acceptance, she did so in the company of someone who was transgender before it was an acceptable option. Surprise indeed!

When working with a medium, spirits provide information about themselves in a variety of ways. If a spirit appears visually, it is easier to tell whether the spirit is male or female. However, appearances can be deceiving. I once met a young female in spirit who dressed like James Dean and called herself Jimmy. Determining the gender of a spirit can be even trickier when the spirit is felt (clairsentience) and not seen. A spirit can be male and yet very sensitive, with a well-developed female side. When dealing with energy—projective (masculine) and receptive (feminine)—a medium quickly learns that a predominance of masculine or feminine energy does not determine gender or sexuality. This is why it is important that a medium receives as much information from a spirit as possible and makes no assumptions.

During our time on Earth, we can be young, old, fathers, mothers, daughters, sons, and more; and, alternately, strong and vulnerable in all of those roles. Spirits are all of these things at the same time rather than over time (only the present moment exists in the afterlife), demonstrating that the essence of each person survives and is greater than the limitations of an earthly body. This is the gift that transsexual and transgender spirits bring.

10. Do you ever receive messages that you don't feel comfortable communicating?

Fortunately, working at the frequency of divine love sidesteps the need for self-censorship. In fact, my deal with spirits is that they are to give me only the information I am to share. Even though it is the sitters who pay me (so it is easy to assume that I answer to them), at the frequency of love, the agenda of the spirits is the priority. Consequently, I trust spirits to know what a sitter is ready to hear and, therefore, don't check in with a sitter at the start of a session to assess what he or she may want to know.

Let me be clear: this doesn't mean that I hold anything back. What it does mean, however, is that I honor the wisdom of the spirits rather than the demands of sitters.

This trust was tested when a brother in spirit named Tyler stated plainly and simply that he had raped his sister when she was eleven. His sister Kim was sitting across from me at the time in a private session. In any context, rape would be a sensitive subject; even so, I shared with Kim that her brother was in the room and what he had said. Kim's eyes flew open, but she stayed seated and acknowledged that she had kept the secret for many years. Tyler expressed deep remorse and provided specific information about Kim that only he would know, including that the rape had caused sexual problems in her marriage.

The next spirit guest was Kim's husband, Bruce, who, while standing with her brother, made it clear that he knew everything that she had suffered in her life. All the secrets were no longer secrets, and he loved her completely.

During our time together, long-held secrets of alcoholism and other addictions were brought into the light as well. At the end of our session, Kim covered her face with her hands and wept. When she could finally speak, she said, "I've waited a lifetime to know I'm loved. And now I know." Had I sidestepped a difficult subject rather than trusted my connection to the spirits, that healing couldn't have happened.

Although this encounter occurred during a private session, spirits are careful not to embarrass audience members by dragging skeletons out of the closet in public. Sometimes, at gallery-style events, I have found myself providing information in some kind of code, using phrases that only family members understand. In situations like this, I let the audience know that they—and I—don't need to know the particulars. (Spirits can be masters of discretion, when necessary.)

As a medium working at the frequency of divine love, I don't worry about what I should or shouldn't say. There is freedom in love—freedom to share and freedom to heal.

> For more on communicating with spirits at the frequency of love, read Q&A number 3, "Is there a difference between a ghost and a spirit?" in chapter 1, "The Basics."

11. Do religious figures such as Mother Mary and Jesus communicate through mediums?

The best way to answer this question is by sharing an experience I had at the Wesak Festival in Mount Shasta, California. It was an encounter with Jesus Christ.

Let me say that Jesus Christ and I weren't strangers. I grew up Christian and, at various times in my life, worshipped in different versions of the Church: Episcopalian when I was young, Catholic prep school in my teens, Evangelical, and then Charismatic denominations in my early twenties. In other words, I went from straitlaced, traditional Christianity to hands-on healing, dancing in the aisles, and speaking in tongues. None of this, however, prepared me for meeting Jesus Christ face to face at the Wesak Festival.

It was the final night of the festival, and I was the last speaker of the weekend. I was exhausted, disoriented, and dressed in clothes just bought with the tags still attached. (My luggage had been lost and I had to run out and buy something to wear.) Simply put, I wasn't at my best.

As I prayed before I got up to speak, I asked for grace and the ability to serve in a way that was better than I felt. When I walked out in front of the crowd, a spotlight hit me square in the face and the audience disappeared. Not only was I temporarily blinded but also I was robbed of one of the primary ways I connect with spirits: clairvoyance. In a desperate plea, I thought, *You have to be extra bright tonight, so I can see you!* With that, a dazzling figure caught my eye, standing at the rear right of the auditorium. The light was almost too bright to bear, so I closed my eyes. Projected onto the screen of my mind was a representation of Jesus—an image that I knew from Saint Mark's Episcopal Church, my childhood church in Yonkers, New York.

When I opened my eyes again, the people sitting around this figure were even more eclipsed by the light emanating from him than from that of the spotlight. Despite the blinding brilliance, I could see the outline of a head, which seemed to be coming from someone sitting taller than the rest in the row. I pointed in the direction of this person and asked, "Does it make sense that I would be seeing Jesus Christ standing next to you?"

"Of course," said a deep masculine voice, as though having Jesus Christ with him was the most natural thing in the world. "As a chiropractor and healer, I work with the Christ consciousness," he continued.

(You and I might have questions about the nature of this working relationship, but neither the man nor Jesus Christ expounded on the subject.)

Next, the sitter's father in spirit, with whom he had a deeply conflicted and disappointing relationship (per the spirit), appeared on the side of the man opposite Jesus Christ. (The father didn't shine as brightly as Christ, but I could still see him.) The father, also a doctor in life, apologized to his son for abandoning him.

The sitter was silent. I couldn't see any reactions on his face, as the light was too bright to see his face at all. And then the father in spirit, after providing me with his name (just to be sure there would be no doubt surrounding his identity), went silent as well. It was then that his son spoke up.

"Yes, I was abandoned by my father—as though I wasn't good enough, as though I was a failure."

Before he could go on, I felt a nudge from the father in spirit (and yes, the nudge felt like physical contact even though he wasn't standing next to me); he had more to say. Pictures of books and a certificate flashed into my mind; and I felt like my chest was blowing up like a balloon—a physical feeling that spirits give me to indicate pride.

"Your father is proud of you," I was able to convey with confidence. And then, above the man's head, I saw "MY SON" in capital letters. My voice rose with emphasis as I said again, "Your father is proud of you. He calls you 'my son.'"

And with that, the message was over.

As I reflected upon this experience for a few days, some thoughts came to mind. It began to make sense that a young man who was following in his father's career footsteps—a young man who also felt abandoned and like a failure—might align himself with Jesus Christ. I was reminded of Jesus's heartfelt cry to God, his father, in the Garden of Gethsemane: "Why have you forsaken me?" This was, in a sense, the same cry of the chiropractor. And yet, at the frequency of love, the father, son, and Jesus Christ were all able to be together in that auditorium in that small town in California.

This extraordinary intersection between the iconic divine and a very human father in spirit makes, in my thinking, an important point: the purpose of my work as a medium isn't at the macro level—to "channel" great wisdom from Christ, Mother Mary, Buddha, or Mohammed; its purpose is to bring healing to everyday sons, daughters, fathers and mothers in an intimate way. It can be hard enough to understand, much less accept, the love of God the Father, but it's even more difficult if your only representative of a father is one who couldn't love. By healing these fundamental human relationships, love can be felt and understood at any level—at least, that's the way it seems to me.

Oh, and by the way, I also think that Jesus Christ appeared as an image I knew from childhood so that I would recognize him. Since all spirits can appear as they choose, so did He. (It is important to note that, by communicating at the frequency of love, there are no posers or imposters, and therefore no need to worry that I was communicating with a Jesus Christ wannabe.)

Jesus Christ isn't the only divine being I've seen and communicated with. Mother Mary, devas, Egyptian gods, and the goddess Diana are just a few of the others I've encountered. There are times when I'm simply awed.

These days, it is quite common to have people in my workshops who align their work with Mother Mary or other religious figures, or who specifically work with the angelic realms. The way I coach a workshop participant to connect with animals in spirit or to channel messages from the Holy Mother is the same way I teach someone to connect with family members. As a teaching medium working at the frequency of love, the function of spirit communication is the same.

To maintain impartiality as a medium, I don't align myself with a particular religion or religious figure. This openness allows messages from loved ones in spirit to come through to all those who are grieving, regardless of their religious backgrounds or beliefs. At the frequency of love, communication is possible with any spirit who matches the frequency. (And for me, that's a *lot* of spirits!)

For more on religious figures, read Q&A number 52, "Do spirits tell you if there's a God?" in chapter 9, "The Big Questions."

12. What's the value of attending a mediumship event?

From its inception, spirit communication has been a group experience. Whether in churches, séances, or public halls, gifted mediums have presented spirits to groups, large and small. In the early days of the work, spirit manifestations were often physical—rapping, table tipping, spirit art (detailed paintings appearing on a canvas without the help of human hands), or slate writing (messages appearing on small blackboards in a deceased person's handwriting). In fact, these physical representations of spirit presences helped to establish Spiritualism as a legitimate religious movement. Modern Spiritualism, which began in the United States in the 1840s, grew in popularity through the Civil War, and then built more momentum through World War I and to the present day. New York's Lily Dale Assembly, founded in 1879, is not only famous for its Spiritualist history but also for providing an immersive environment in which prominent mediums counsel and teach.

Today's mediums often work outside of Spiritualist churches and organizations, and use books, TV, and the internet to share spirit messages with thousands—even millions—of people, sometimes simultaneously. As impersonal as these electronic events may seem, loved ones in spirit can still guide or inspire a person in the audience to hear a specific, heart-healing message. The major difference between a broadcast event and a live demonstration is not the size of the audience but the impact of a shared in-person experience. You can think of it this way: an in-person demonstration differs from a TV event just like attending a live concert differs from watching a concert on TV. Demonstrations of mediumship, also called gallery-style events, are the largest of all in-person events.

The purpose of a demonstration is for people to see how a particular medium works. Everyone in attendance is part of the experience whether he or she receives a personal message or not. At a demonstration, we can feel the presence of spirits as well as share the emotions of others in the room. That's what makes an in-person experience— even one in a large group—different from any other.

Another reason I enjoy presenting larger events is that they provide an opportunity for people who are intrigued by but wary about spirit communication to experience it in a safe and comfortable setting. Many people attend group events thinking, *I'll just watch* (though that's not what always happens!). One of the anomalies of a group situation is that those who may not be expecting (or even wanting) a message get one anyway. I always find this amusing, as do the friends who dragged the surprised person along to the event. This happens because of the way energy works, not because spirits are contrarians. As I often say, "There are no observers at events; we're all participants."

At a group event, my spirit guides manage my energy and the energy of the crowd in the most effective way. This allows as many people as possible to receive a message in the least depleting way for me. It's also why a personal message for one person may be meaningful to a person sitting all the way across the room as well. During the introduction to any group event, I always explain: "As much as I would like to convey a personal message to each and every one of you, that isn't physically possible. However, spirits know how to touch the greatest number of people with each message given, so listen carefully—there will be a message for you!"

After a recent event, a young woman said to me, "When you told the lady in the front row that her mother would be attending her upcoming wedding, I felt as though my mother was telling me the same thing. I'm getting married in a month, and I was hoping that my mother would be there." In this manner, spirits choose to share one message that will touch many in the audience.

From my experience, audience members who arrive without expectations and maintain an attitude of anticipation and gratitude make it easier for spirits to make contact. Each participant's energy impacts what spirits are able to accomplish during a demonstration, making extraordinary things happen because of the collective energy in the room.

At one gallery-style event, as I continued to address the audience while walking down the center aisle, I came to a sudden stop; it felt as though a hand was pressed to my chest. "I just heard the word suicide as I reached this area," I said, and a number of people raised their hands.

A male in spirit standing between two women caught my eye. The energy link between the women was so strong that I assumed they knew each other. To my surprise, that wasn't the case. However, when I mentioned the name Anna, the two women both acknowledged the name as their own. They each knew a male who had died by suicide, and the similarities were startling. After much evidence was shared, the spirit standing directly behind the Anna with dark hair said, "I come to you with hummingbirds."

"Yes, I know," she replied.

"Don't get the tattoo!" he shouted in my ear, and I shouted out in relay.

"Too late—I already did!" Anna shouted in return, rolling up her sleeve to reveal a larger-than-life hummingbird tattoo.

Of course, the spirit—her son—knew this, but he still made the statement to great effect. The audience erupted in laughter, and Anna joined in. After several minutes of mirth and demands that the tattoo be displayed for all to see, the spirits moved me to another section of the ballroom.

Following the event, the two Annas came together to speak with me. They were astonished not only by the fact that they were both named Anna but also by the fact that the loved ones they had lost to suicide were both named Nick. It was my turn to be awestruck!

Later, I received messages from both Annas. Here is what they said, in part:

> I am one of the Annas. (We sat next to each other, even though we didn't know each other.) You talked to both of us. I knew that [my Nick] wanted to talk to me, and I wouldn't have known about this event or come to it if it wasn't for him pointing me that way.[4]

* * *

> I am the "other" Anna, the one with the hummingbird tattoo. I originally sat several rows back and, at the last minute, decided to move up. There was a vacant seat between two women, and I took it. Two [Annas]—complete strangers, seated next to each other, with the same first name, [who] both lost a loved one in the exact same manner, . . . [two] loved ones [who] also have the same first name![5]

What I love about these messages is that the Annas make an important point: they were each guided by their own Nicks to attend the event, to sit next to each other, and ultimately, to meet and have a conversation—proof that spirit communication is a coordinated, cooperative experience. It isn't all up to the medium!

Spirits use the power of resonance to inspire comfort and an alliance of healing. For these two women in particular, the abandonment and isolation felt by those who have survived the suicide of a loved one was counterbalanced by their instant connection. I have no doubt that the two Nicks in spirit were delighted when it was revealed that they shared the same name. (And spirits love pulling stunts like that!)

But what I think is most valuable about the spirits' use of resonance is this: spirits can use one message to heal many. This healing energy moves us all away from the isolating cry of despair—"Me, me, me . . ." It allows us to feel and acknowledge the empowering and inclusive "me *too*" connection with others. In essence, during a group event, we can all walk away with more hope and joy than the grief and despair that accompanied us on the way in.

In powerful moments of resonance, shared grief is transformed into shared healing—a validation that those we love in spirit are not only with us but interacting with us in the physical world. That is what a spirit-inspired communal experience is all about. As a medium, it is helpful for spirits to use resonance to effect the greatest possible change within the limits of time and available energy. Spirits are effective energy managers; I've learned that by following their lead, the path of least resistance provides the greatest return.

At that event, on that day, all of us present *did* receive a message thanks to Anna and Anna and Nick and Nick. And the message was simple and universal: life is a shared event, and you are not alone.

13. Is an in-person session with a medium more effective than a phone session?

When deciding whether to schedule an in-person or a phone session with a medium, it might help to understand how each experience is different for the spirits, the medium, and the sitter.

As far as spirits are concerned, there is no difference between connecting during an in-person session or over the phone. Why is this? Spirits aren't limited by distance, and they can be present in more than one place at a time. In other words, a spirit can provide information to me in California while standing next to the sitter in Minnesota. The fact that spirits are not location based is what allows me to provide messages on radio shows for listeners who call in, or via Zoom or online forums. Fortunately, the only spirits I see and connect with in these forums are those related to the callers. If this weren't the case, a confusing, chaotic free-for-all would be the result!

Something to keep in mind is that spirits love technology and will often manipulate it to announce their presence. High-frequency, intense spirit energy can actually be disruptive during remote sessions, causing dropped calls, finicky recordings, and computer glitches. This is one of the reasons why I no longer record phone sessions—I was being blamed for bad recordings! Fortunately, when people record their own sessions, there are fewer difficulties, because it isn't the same device being exposed to spirit energy repeatedly. For phone sessions, it is also suggested that people use a landline or cell service, with all bars (good reception), a full charge, and a charger handy. Spirit energy can also quickly run down batteries!

Aside from the technical challenges for the medium, phone sessions are just as effective as in-person sessions, with the same information received, but the interaction between spirits and sitters is different. During phone sessions, there are fewer distractions all around; it is just the spirits and the medium, and a voice on the phone. During in-person sessions, however, there is more of a dual focus. This doesn't mean that the medium is multitasking but rather adapting to a relational difference. For instance, when I'm sitting with a sitter, spirits congregate in a certain way around the sitter, which indicates their relationship to the sitter and one another. When speaking by phone, spirits will present themselves in other identifying ways (for instance, clairsentience [a spirit who feels like a father] or clairalience [a spirit who comes with a smell, like Old Spice]). Adapting the methods of receiving information allows for clear communication, whether the medium is face-to-face with a sitter or speaking by phone half a world away.

The spirits' and the medium's abilities to adapt is good news for people whose only option is a phone session. Because my client base is worldwide, connecting by phone is not only an effective way to receive messages but also a cost-effective way to conserve the medium's energy. It isn't physically possible for me to fly to every part of the world, although, judging from my schedule, I'm trying!

Therefore, if in-person and phone sessions are equally effective from the standpoint of the spirits and the medium, why do people consistently choose to meet with a medium in person? To find out, I've asked several clients to explain why:

"I wanted to meet with you first. I wanted to feel comfortable with you and wanted a good connection," said one woman who flew from Iowa in hopes of hearing from her son in spirit. After our first session together, she scheduled subsequent appointments by phone. Her feedback made me realize that part of the connection that sitters want to feel is with the medium. Because loved ones in spirit can seem ephemeral, it is comforting to be in the presence of a person who is acting as an intermediary.

One sitter said, "It was like visiting with my mother and a friend," emphasizing how having a connection with me, the medium (i.e., the friend), was an important part of the experience. Another sitter exclaimed in the middle of her session, "Your face changed, and you suddenly looked exactly like my sister!" Although I hadn't become her sister, spirits can overlay their energy onto my face, a process called transmogrification.

It is quite common for the energy of spirits to affect people when they're in the room with me as well. "I thought someone touched my hand," reported a young woman as I was speaking with her mother, who had recently passed. A desire for a tactile experience is often another reason people prefer an in-person session with a medium.

I've recently begun offering sessions and small circles via online video conferencing. This option combines the face-to-face experience of an in-person session with the convenience of a phone session. The energy of spirit communication can affect computers and other equipment (sudden battery loss and so on), but fortunately, high-speed internet and sophisticated electronics are proving to be able to withstand the vibrations.

When weighing the pros and cons of an in-person, phone, or video-conferencing appointment, the question to ask is, "What would create the most memorable visit?" If there are physical limitations, know that the spirits and the medium will be completely and absolutely present for you via phone or computer. However, if you desire the chance to watch the medium interact with your loved ones and possibly feel the energy of the spirits yourself, an in-person session might be the way to go.

Either way, loved ones in spirit are ready and determined to make the connection. They are far less concerned about the logistics and more interested in letting you know that their love for you continues.

14. Is mediumship exhausting work?

The intense energy at larger events is usually obvious as I connect with spirits throughout a crowd. Some energies (of people and spirits) are denser than others and may impact me physically as connections are made. In this sense, spirit communication is a full contact sport! In addition, during events, which can last a couple of hours, I stand and move about (sometimes quite quickly). So yes, a lot of energy is expended, which can be exhausting, but that is only part of the story.

There are three participants in every spirit message: the spirit, the sitter, and the medium. Even in large auditoriums, each person in the audience is a participant; there are no observers. If you're sitting in the room, you're part of the experience—*everyone* is a sitter.

This was made crystal clear during an online reading at a live event. The woman I could see on the screen didn't recognize the spirit I described. Suddenly, I heard a voice off-screen say, "That's my dad." A skeptical husband, accompanying his wife, was sitting in the room as an observer and had been reluctant to acknowledge his (and his father's) presence. When you're in the room, you're *in*, as far as the spirits are concerned!

The third part of the communication equation is the medium. Mediums who are serious about their work will practice diligently to master the craft. One of the aspects of mediumship I pay careful attention to is energy management. At the frequency of love, the spirits and I have a clear, high vibrational link; however, the people who come to an event, a circle, or a private session may be deep in grief and grievance (resentment about something that is perceived to be wrong or unfair, such as the murder of a loved one).

Being an empath, as most mediums are (highly sensitive people who can read as well as take on the emotional burdens of others), I could be greatly affected by the pain of the people who come to see me. If I sit in the pain and despair of my sitters, I can offer them person-to-person solace and comfort but run the risk of becoming drained. If I align myself with the frequency of love with the spirits, however, I become detached from the pain and energized by love. In this state, during the course of a session, I've watched as clients also become attuned to the frequency of love; and the pain of their grief begins to dissipate. The biggest energy (love) wins out!

Even so, being a conduit for spirit messages via the powerful frequency of love can be exhausting. That is why I have developed helpful energy-management practices and habits. I limit the number of events and private sessions that I do each day, for example—this is why I don't "squeeze in" extra sittings. But in addition, I watch where I expend my energy on a daily basis and engage in calming practices, such as meditation and walks in nature. Spirit communication is also a thirsty business, so I tend to drink lots of water. Good eating habits, which include eating more plants than meat and more complex carbohydrates than sugary desserts are a plus as well. I almost always have a pack of almonds in my purse to keep energy high and hunger at bay.

When I've overextended myself, I've gotten a headache in the center of my head, which seems to me to be the nexus of clairvoyance and the crown chakra. When I've overused clairaudience, my voice has, on occasion, given out entirely. And stomach upsets are an indication that I've depended too much on my psychic sense to navigate through the world.

As I mentioned before, most mediums are empaths, and as a teacher of spirit communication, I have lots of firsthand experience working with highly sensitive people. Many have come to me overwhelmed and overcome by their sensitivities, and exhausted by the demands of others (explicit or implicit) to fix a situation or make someone else feel better. I've been there and know what it is like to think that your sole purpose in life is to make everyone *else* feel better!

But there is a different way: I can share some simple things I've learned to do (and still practice) to maintain and conserve my personal energy so that I am available to serve the spirits. Although these practices can be helpful for everyone, they are especially useful for anyone who identifies as an empath. If you are interested in being a spirit communicator, these practices will also prepare you for managing the energies of the work.

Here are some of the things we all can do to protect ourselves from what may be draining our energy.

Pay attention.

Notice if you feel exhausted in certain situations or when you're with certain people, especially if it happens repeatedly. At first, it can be easy to miss the link between a situation or person and feelings of being drained, because the effects might not show up immediately. It can also be helpful to check in with a friend or family member who knows you well.

For example, a friend of mine (who is a medium and healer) asked for my help when she noticed that visiting with a mutual friend became exhausting time and again. When we all met for what was meant to be a relaxing evening, I saw a small tube of light between my two friends— with energy moving in only one direction. Fortunately, we were all able to discuss the situation with honesty and compassion, which isn't always possible or easy to do. What we came to understand was that our mutual friend was going through a difficult time taking care of her mother, who was incapacitated. She herself was exhausted and, unknowingly, was draining energy from friends who were open and giving people (and empaths). During our conversation, we discussed ways for her to take care of herself to conserve and build her own energy.

Stay grounded and protected.

Grounding and protection meditations and simple practices like walking in nature can help us remain connected to Earth's energy and protected from negative, energy-sapping influences. Forest bathing (walking through a forest meditatively, allowing the energy of nature to ground and heal you) has become quite popular recently. If you aren't near trees or are unable to walk in nature, a great substitute is an easy grounding and protection meditation like this one:

* Sit in a straight-backed chair, with your feet on the ground and your hands on your lap.

* Imagine yourself at the base of a tree, with your back to the tree and your feet at the roots.

* Become aware of your breathing and follow your breath gently: in and out, in and out.

* Imagine roots growing from the base of your spine and the bottoms of your feet into the earth, entwining with the roots of the tree.

* Allow yourself to feel heavy, drawn close to the earth.

* As you sit quietly, allow the earth's energy to move up through your roots. It may be helpful to think of this energy as sap or water.

* Imagine that the branches and leaves of the tree are sheltering you, protecting you, reaching down to hug you.

* Allow yourself to sit in this space and in this energy, noticing any differences in the way you feel.

* Once you feel grounded, protected, and peaceful, visualize your roots gently falling off your body and feel yourself sitting in your chair once again.

* Get up slowly from the chair, turn to face it, and, standing at the foot of your imagined tree, say, "Thank you."

Set boundaries.

Good-hearted people who desire to help others may find it difficult to say no to anything asked of them. During a recent session, a mother in spirit wrote "no" in huge letters over what looked like an office building. The spirit flashed a child's drawing of a family into my mind as well. Her daughter confirmed that she had recently turned down extra projects at work, which had been interfering with family time. Self-care and recognizing personal limitations are important to all of us, mediums included. As previously mentioned, working as a medium can be energy intensive, so I limit the number of sessions I schedule each day and how many events are scheduled each month.

Be empowered.

Spend time doing things that strengthen your energy (i.e., cooking healthy meals, exercising, doing yoga, meditating). Practice gratitude to lessen the negative effect of grievances on your well-being. Practice self-compassion, which frees up energy attached to regrets and past mistakes. Check in with yourself and your energy level on a regular basis, and take steps to recharge your battery. Take a nap. Go for a walk. Chat with an old friend. Read a good book.

Seek reciprocity.

Imagine what your life would be like if you were able to not only give as you receive but also receive as you give. Foster relationships with people who encourage and support you in the same manner as you support them. Allow people to give to you freely and selflessly. (This isn't always easy for people who are "helpers.") Enjoy the caring company of animals and nature.

* * *

As the demands of our lives increase and we feel pulled in many directions, it is more important than ever to be good stewards of our personal energy systems. By paying attention, staying grounded, setting boundaries, being empowered, and seeking reciprocity, we safeguard our life force; and by doing so, we fuel our intention for powerful results.

15. Do mediums like or dislike cemeteries?

I live next to a cemetery. Some people may assume that I choose to live by a cemetery because I'm a medium (which isn't the case), or that I'm constantly visited by the recently deceased (which I'm not). However, throughout my life, I've been drawn to these and other "cities of the dead." As a teenager, I had what some might have thought an odd interest in reading gravestones. While in Europe, I was entranced by gravestone rubbing and rubbed until my arms could no longer move. In looking back, I realized that I cared about the people who were "gone," even if they had been deceased for centuries. I was curious about their lives and loves; I wanted to know about them. It's not surprising, I guess, that I became a medium.

These days, I appreciate the cemetery next door as a lovely place to walk. The trees are old—older than the cemetery itself—and the grounds are beautifully kept, with fountains, rose gardens, and park benches. No gravestones mar the sightlines, and at times, the only reminder that it is a cemetery are the flowers left in remembrance or the chairs set up under an awning in preparation for a service.

The grounds are quite extensive. One morning, I found myself wandering toward a section that isn't in my usual walking path. Glancing around, I saw more flowers and plants than usual; and balloons, pinwheels, and teddy bears—I was standing among the graves of children. At each decorated gravesite, I looked at the plaques, pausing at one with a "Hello Kitty" logo inscribed next to the pictures of two young faces. "What could have taken you two so suddenly?" my curious nature asked. As I sat quietly on a nearby bench, I didn't hear any young ones in spirit speaking with me, though I'm not surprised. Without a doubt, they were with their families, enjoying their company as they did in life, as children in spirit do.

Walking back through the cemetery toward my car, I considered the idea that my attraction to cemeteries is more than curiosity about lives lived; spending time in cemeteries reminds me that death and life are partners. Not only isn't there one without the other but also each encourages us to appreciate the other. Walking in the midst of death reminds me to be more alive on Earth.

While providing messages from loved ones in spirit, I am constantly looking at life from the perspective of the spirits. They view themselves as involved in life on Earth and, at the same time, living expansively beyond it. For example, at an event in northern California, a young man in spirit provided his name, described his life, and introduced relatives in spirit that he hadn't met while on Earth. He explained that he finally understood how he fit into the ancestral line, even though he hadn't felt part of the family while on Earth. His life on Earth finally made sense. For spirits, death isn't a separation or limitation; it is an all-access pass to understanding.

Looking at life from a spirit perspective can make the details of life on Earth seem tiresome at best. As one lady said at a book-signing event, "The afterlife sounds so great that I just want to get there." However, as spirits remind us time and again, it is what we think and do in our lives *here* that helps create our lives there; it is in the details of life that love is expressed. The very limitations of life (including a literal "drop dead" deadline) spur us on to take action.

The illusion of the dualities of life and death, heaven and earth, being and doing, limitation and expansion is the very thing that calls us to live life like a spirit now. Why not live expansive lives while we're here? As I travel and meet people from around the world, it seems as though many are choosing to do just that.

After returning from the walk in my neighboring cemetery, I was compelled to call Sondra, who has been my friend since the fifth grade. She lives in Boston. As we talked about her socially conscious and active church (Unitarian), we laughed that the congregation balked at renaming the annual Easter Egg Hunt as the Spring Egg Hunt (a more politically correct appellation). The Unitarian Church's (not renamed) Easter Egg Hunt is staged in a local historic cemetery in which pastel-colored eggs are hidden among the tombstones. Every year, children run over graves with screeches of delight as they find hidden treasures and their baskets begin to fill.

After hanging up with Sondra, I reflected upon the slightly bizarre picture of an Easter-egg hunt in a cemetery. In actuality, the message of Easter and spring are well placed in a cemetery, merging the idea of life surviving death with the celebration of new life in spring.

So, I've decided that I'm going to live my life like a kid in a cemetery, filling my basket with the most beautiful Easter eggs I can find. Won't you join me?

3

The Dying Experience

16. Do spirits visit those who are dying?

As people move closer to death, especially if there's been a health crisis, they can become aware of loved ones in spirit who have already passed. This serves a twofold purpose: first, loved ones in spirit can help the person dying to be at peace with the process; and second, it is a personal invitation to take the next step in life. In essence, the presence of spirits is much more than a visit—it is a welcoming reunion.

It is common for someone nearing death to call out the names of loved ones in spirit. For instance, a brother in spirit mentioned the name "Toto" during a session, and I saw a little black dog in spirit with him.

"Oh, my brother's last word was *Toto*," said his sister. "We hoped our childhood dog was there to meet him." (I was very much relieved that there was an actual Toto in spirit and I wasn't experiencing a weird, metaphysical *Wizard of Oz* moment.)

During a Zoom session, I was enjoying a visit with a loving wife named Leila and Richard, her husband in spirit. After presenting a number of specific details of his life (including his hobbies, his favorite snacks, and names of friends and relatives), Richard made it clear that he hadn't wanted to die in a hospital, and he got his wish: "Richard wanted to be near a window; he wanted to see outside. He wanted to see the birds," I shared with Leila.

"Yes, he loved seeing into the backyard, which was filled with crows. It was an amazing sight!" Leila confirmed.

Richard continued his message by mentioning that his mother was with him while he was dying. Leila gasped and then told me that during her husband's final hours, he turned his head and kept staring toward one corner of the ceiling. Even when Leila or his daughters called his name, he refused to turn his head away from that one part of the room. Leila was hoping that her husband was seeing his beloved mother, and she was relieved to receive confirmation.

Leila also reported that, to this day, there is a discoloration—a yellowed area—on the ceiling, where Richard was staring. (Spirits can alter temperatures from hot to cold, so I suspect that the concentration of energy heated the spot where the spirit remained present for Richard; and that is the reason for the paint's change in color.) No one in Leila's family is willing to paint over that spot. It serves as a physical reminder that Richard's mother was present well in advance of the moment of his death.

So yes, spirits visit those who are dying, and those who are dying can see them—and in fact, may not be able to take their eyes off them!

17. If I don't get to say goodbye before I die, is it too late to do so after?

"Your father is giving me the sense that you weren't with him when he died," I told a woman who had been identified by her father in spirit as "Daddy's girl."

"Yes, that's right," she replied.

"My head is feeling woozy, so my sense is that your father was on serious pain medication just before he passed," I continued.

"Yes, he was on a morphine drip at the end."

"Now I'm smelling tuna fish and seeing a tuna-fish sandwich. Were you getting a tuna-fish sandwich when he died?"

"Yes, actually," she replied, starting to show emotion, which, up to that point, she had been trying to hide. "I was hungry and went to the hospital cafeteria. I got a tuna melt and ate it there so that it wouldn't smell up my dad's room. By the time I returned, he had died."

✳ ✳ ✳

A mother in spirit said to her daughter, Elvia, who had cared for her during a long illness, "Thank you for telling me that it was okay for me to go."

Elvia confirmed that as she sat at her mother's death-bed, she told her, "Mom, it's okay; I'll be fine." And within hours, her mother passed.

These are just a couple of end-of-life scenarios in which loved ones were nearby at the point of death, but the results were quite different: one brought intense feelings of self-doubt and the other a feeling of completion. It can be extremely painful when a loved one dies suddenly and there isn't an opportunity for that final conversation, that final goodbye.

During my years of working with spirits and their families, I've tracked the percentage of deaths where a loved one was present and where a loved one was not. Interestingly enough, it is about 50/50. (Keep in mind that this is not scientific research but an informal assessment.)

For those of you who have felt suddenly left behind, I've got a secret to share: sometimes people die suddenly or without the presence of those they love because it is easier for them to leave the body this way. And despite the pain of losing loved ones in this manner, spirits can be surprisingly matter of fact about it, as I learned when speaking with a client named Yasmine.

In the middle of Yasmine's session, her mother in spirit gave me the sense that she had died abruptly, without her daughter in the room.

"You weren't able to be with your mother when she died, were you?" I asked Yasmine.

She burst into tears and said with a bitter tone, "She died twenty minutes after I left."

"I had to go when I did," her mother responded.

"That's just what the nurse said," replied Yasmine.

"It is easy to think that your mother's passing at that time was because she was angry," I said to Yasmine.

"Yes," she admitted. "It really felt like that—as though her choosing to die without me there was meant to hurt me."

"Well, your mother's telling me that dead people aren't attractive."

This elicited a laugh from Yasmine, who said that her mother hated to see dead people—she wouldn't go to wakes or funerals for that reason.

"Your mother didn't want you to see her dead in bed. She wants you to think of her as alive and well."

The dead *are* alive; and in this sense, it's never too late to say *anything*. A medium isn't required for communicating with someone on the other side, and there is no need to worry about your message not being received. When we use someone's name in our thoughts and prayers, the sound of the name carries the message—the name of a person is a powerful link. In fact, a respected medium I know asks sitters to speak their first names aloud at the start of a session. Think of it this way: when you're at a crowded party, if someone mentions your name across the room, you're alerted, despite the music and other conversation. It is much the same way with spirits.

Remember that admonition "Don't speak ill of the dead?" Well, implicit in that statement is the understanding that the dead *do* indeed hear us. And often, they need to hear what we weren't able to say to them in life, whether it's positive or what we may think is negative. It is never too late to say, "I love you" or "I'm sorry" or "I'm angry with you." It is never too late to give or receive forgiveness. These opportunities do not end with what we call death. And don't worry; whatever needs saying, spirits can handle it!

One final thought: it is preferable to keep current with all relationships while you're on Earth. If you love somebody, make sure they know it. If you need to set things right with someone, do it now. As a medium, much of my work involves expressing the regrets of loved ones in spirit and of sitters for what they have or haven't done, and remorse for the pain they've caused. The less I have to do this, the better!

For more on connecting with loved ones in spirit, read Q&A number 30, "Do spirits know how much we love and miss them?" in chapter 5, "Afterlife Relationships."

18. Can a spirit leave the body before the body actually dies?

The simple answer to this question is yes. However, the explanation of this simple yes could take pages and pages to explain, and in fact, *has.* Numerous books have been written about the separation of spirit (consciousness) from the physical body, including bestselling books about near-death experiences, like those by Dr. Eben Alexander and Anita Moorjani, as well as books about astral projection and consciousness research.

Not that long ago, death was more definitive; however, these days, that isn't the case. The exact time of death has become more difficult to determine because medical support can keep the physical body alive without any discernible brain activity. Physician, clinical researcher, and author Haider Warraich tackles this tough subject in his book *Modern Death: How Medicine Changed the End of Life.* In this well-researched book, Warraich traces how the dying process has changed drastically during the last hundred years.

Although Warraich approaches the subject from a physician's point of view and I come from a metaphysical point of view, we both are asking the same questions: When exactly is a person dead? Where is the consciousness of a person who is in a persistent vegetative state? Does death release the spirit, or do the body and consciousness act independently from one another? Can a spirit leave the body before the body actually dies? Where is consciousness created and where does consciousness reside—in the brain or outside of it?

What consciousness is and where it resides creates a number of challenges, sometimes confusing mediums. I've experienced these perplexing conundrums myself. Imagine my surprise when I once discovered that a lovely spirit dressed impeccably in a blue floral dress and hat *wasn't* dead! When she said "Alzheimer's" in my ear, her daughter confirmed that her mother was alive with the disease but hadn't been able to communicate with her family for eight years!

At another event, I spoke with a loving mother in spirit (or rather, I *thought* she was in spirit) who was outlining for her daughter the difficulties she and her siblings were facing. All the information presented was true and accurate, including discussions held in her room. To find out that these conversations were taking place *while* she was in a coma was enough to cause me to hyperventilate! Up to that point, I hadn't spoken with a person in a coma—this was a first! And it struck at the core of who I identified myself to be: a medium who only speaks to *spirits*—people who are dead!

As much as I shy away from making a habit of speaking with spirits whose bodies are breathing (on a ventilator or otherwise), these situations bring up real questions. With the ability to keep bodies alive indefinitely, is that the best option? Some people take the legal steps before an emergency arises by signing a do-not-resuscitate (DNR) order, but DNRs aren't always completed, especially by people who don't think that death is near, like young people.

Since much of my experience with spirits is with the young who have passed, I naturally turn to them when thinking about the final separation of body and spirit. There is often a sudden severing of physical life with the young—deaths that may seem not only tragic but also traumatic. One young man in spirit told me about being catapulted out of his body when his car hit a tree at 95 miles per hour. Another young man in spirit showed me an image of himself standing outside of his body, watching while his body was running and burning. (He had caught on fire during a fireworks-display accident.) To his surviving parents, who were present, it seemed as though he was burning alive and in terrible pain. To their relief, his version of events made it clear that he was not suffering.

A dear friend, who fell off a balcony in France and subsequently died without regaining consciousness, shared with me from spirit that he stood on the balcony and watched himself fall—he was already out of his body. This was a great comfort to me because I'd imagined that he must have felt the impact of his body hitting the cobblestones.

Spirits speak of a tremendous grace at the time of death. Those of us left behind, however, may imagine how someone must have suffered during a horrific death. At the end of life, when someone is struggling to breathe, we may think that perhaps that person doesn't want to die and is fighting to stay. Instead, consider the possibility that the body is just doing what it is supposed to do—provide a living vehicle for the spirit. Once the spirit vacates that vehicle, the body can finally let go. Spirits will often correct our versions of their deaths to let us know that the experience wasn't how it looked, and that their passing was far easier than we envisioned.

I have discovered this to also be true with those living life with diminishing cognition as well. Not once has someone who has either passed with Alzheimer's or is living with it given me a sense that they felt trapped in a body with a brain that couldn't respond. My dad once asked what the value might be of his visits to a friend who no longer recognized him. I reminded him that spirits have shared with me the details of visits from loved ones, even when it seemed as though they had no cognizance of what was going on around them. When I speak with spirits who had Alzheimer's, dementia, or who were in a coma, they have conveyed astonishing details of family visits, gifts brought by visitors, and conversations held both inside and outside of their rooms! Consciousness and memory are *not* limited by brainpower, and both survive bodily death. The people we love exist fully and completely whether the body is functional or not. No act of kindness toward them goes unnoticed; all acts of love are appreciated. In other words, we can take all memories with us even if the brain isn't able to function to capacity!

As you can see, a simple question like the one asked here can raise many other questions. I don't claim to know all the answers, but I am willing to explore the mysteries of consciousness and spirit. Medicine, technology, and metaphysics may very well intersect in a powerful way in the ever-broadening space between life and death.

19. When multiple people die at the same time, do they share the dying experience?

The pain of losing someone we love can be compounded by the circumstances of the passing. Grief increases exponentially when more than one person passes at the same time, especially when they're related. My first experience of a multiple-family-member passing occurred during a gallery-style event in a small town in northern California. During my opening remarks, three young people in spirit (two boys and a girl) appeared. When it came time for messages from the spirits, these three spoke together, a bit like a Greek chorus.

"Fast, fast, fast," they said, about the way they had lived and the way they had died. They showed me a picture of the tree their car struck. They reported no pain and no fear, and they assured their mothers (who were sisters) that they were together and would be standing behind their parents—*always*.

In another memorable spirit visit, three young children introduced themselves by name and stood hand in hand. Each one, in turn, told me that they had dreamed their way through the dying process. (They were siblings who had passed during the night from CO_2 poisoning.) Judy, the smallest of the three, enthusiastically talked about her baby brother, who had survived. (He had been born only three months before she died, and Judy had treated him like a prized doll.) As each child spoke to their mother and grandmother, their love and enthusiasm for life (and the afterlife) began to soften the hard edge of unbearable grief. I learned later from their grandmother that the day following our session by phone was the first time her daughter (their mother) had gotten out of bed in the morning and stayed so all day. Up to that point, her grief had been so debilitating that she remained in bed most of the day.

When I picked up the phone one afternoon, I heard *Bang! Bang! Bang!* signifying three gunshots. Two young boys in spirit were present, but they were so full of energy and moving so quickly that it was hard to get a good look at them. Their mother confirmed that there had been three gunshots on the day they died. Their father had killed the boys and then turned the gun on himself. The boys told me that they had died quickly; the older passed first, and he was right there for his younger brother when he died too. What struck me most of all was that the violence and betrayal didn't seem to have affected them at all. They shared their love of Beatles' music (John Lennon made a brief appearance in spirit) and acknowledged that they were helping their mother with a foundation she created to promote nonviolence. The boys' mother said that "Imagine" by John Lennon was their favorite song.

In the middle of the session, several representatives in spirit from the father's family made an appearance, expressing deep regret for the pain caused by him. These relatives, whom the mother knew, made it clear that the boys had not seen their father since their passing. This was a great comfort to their mother, who had been terrified to think otherwise. The family in spirit told me that the father was in a different place. In this case, even though all three had passed at almost the same time, they did not end up together.

Some of you may be wondering if the father wasn't with the children he killed, where was he? The spirits that communicated with me during the session didn't provide an address to his afterlife relocation. His family, however, was still connected to him *and* to his sons. In this way, there is a possible bridge or link between the *entire* family.

This may be unsettling to some who would prefer there to be eternal damnation for those who commit heinous acts. Perfect justice does exist—all deeds come to light and must be faced, and personal responsibility accepted. But as I've come to learn from the spirits, the pathway to forgiveness, healing, wholeness, and love is open to *all*. There is always a possibility of reconciliation once a soul can match the frequencies of love, joy, and peace. The comfort for those who have survived or died during terrible bouts of violence is that, until a matching of those frequencies is possible, there isn't a meeting between the victim(s) and the aggressor(s). In other words, spirits who may have suffered on Earth at the hands of another don't randomly come face to face with that abuser in the afterlife.

As a postscript, I'd like to add that a couple of years after first meeting these two boys, I had the chance to speak with them again, when their mother set up a phone session. After getting reacquainted, they showed me wedding bells. I heard the bells ringing and saw it as a symbol for an upcoming wedding. The boys seemed excited about this wedding. At this point, their mother told me that the reason she called was because she was getting remarried and wanted to be sure that her boys were okay with it. Of course they knew, and they let me in on a secret: their mother was marrying the police officer who was called to the scene of their deaths.

In each of these cases, the interest of those who had passed was to make clear that they weren't eternally scarred by the way they had passed. The most important message by far was the reaffirming that their loving relationships with each other remained intact and their connections to loved ones on Earth remained strong.

20. Do spirits still feel the physical pain associated with their deaths?

The short answer to this question is no. However, now that you've heaved a sigh of relief, I'd like to answer in a more detailed way.

As a medium, my job requirements include providing as much evidence as possible that I am speaking to a specific person in spirit. That evidence frequently includes the way a person has died. For example, at a recent event, two men in spirit—a husband and boyfriend—stood behind a woman in the group. She didn't seem at all surprised or uncomfortable with their presence. What surprised me, though, was the level of interaction between the two spirits.

The boyfriend announced that he had died after months of life-energy-sapping kidney failure. "It wasn't a manly enough way to die," he declared.

With that, his companion, the sitter's first husband, blurted out "prostate cancer!" which was not only a contributing factor of his death but also definitely "manly." His wife and the rest of the group found this tête-à-tête amusing, to say the least.

A light-hearted approach to illness and death doesn't deny the pain and suffering of illnesses that eventually separate the spirit from the body. Instead, it highlights the fact that the "evidence," whether it's cancer, a car accident, or a gunshot, is, for the spirit, nothing more than a memory. Spirits aren't re-experiencing pain when they provide evidence, nor do they carry these physical feelings with them into the afterlife. Spirits don't have dense physical bodies, so there aren't joints and organs to be affected any longer by pain after death. In fact, *all* physical suffering passes away, including any limitations caused by brain malfunctioning. In the afterlife, physical challenges like intellectual disability, autism, bipolar disease, and Alzheimer's do not exist.

Another reason that spirits share their death condition with a medium is to dispel assumptions about their dying process. "It looked much worse than it was!" a loving father in spirit proclaimed when describing his gasping for breath in the final hour of his life. Although we on Earth may be understandably concerned about the way a person dies, spirits can seem oddly detached from their own death experiences. When someone we love dies, we can be left with the shock and trauma of their last moments—as though a door has slammed in our faces, with little explanation. However, for those who have died, the door simply closed on physical pain and opened to an unfettered world of peace.

Many spirits have shared with me that their deaths were the way they wanted them to be, even if their dying process seemed "wrong" to those they left behind. "I died doing what I loved," a young man in spirit said as he showed me a helicopter and beautiful snowcapped mountains. His mother confirmed that her son had died in an avalanche while heli-skiing. In my experience with spirits, they talk less about how they died and far more about how they lived on Earth, and how they remain connected to us.

Rest assured: spirits are freed of pain (physical, emotional, and mental). Just as they have peace about the way they died, we can as well.

21. What happens to people who commit suicide?

My beautiful cousin, Tommy, shot and killed himself on a Thanksgiving eve years ago. It is because of this painful experience that I have tremendous empathy for those living in the tumultuous wake of a suicide.

There is a persistent belief that people who die from suicide are treated differently in the afterlife. This could explain why spirits who have passed by suicide appear to speak with me with such frequency. They want their loved ones to know that they have not only survived suicide but also that they are not in limbo or living in hell. This point was made with great impact when I was meeting with a mother whose son, a former altar boy, had hanged himself. She stood in the doorway of my office and without preamble said, "My priest told me that my son is condemned, and we will be separated from God and each other forever."

This left me momentarily speechless, but upon recovering, I asked, "Well then, why are you here?"

She responded without pause, "I didn't like what the priest said, so I want a second opinion." This dedicated mother refused to believe that God's love for her son wasn't as big as her own.

The great irony of suicide is that death doesn't solve the problems of life—or inure anyone to the impact of choices made on Earth. But fortunately, love *is* bigger than suicide. And because it is, those who pass as a result of suicide can face and fully understand the ramifications of their actions—the suicide itself, as well as the beliefs and choices leading to their final act on Earth.

During a Zoom session, this point was reiterated by a former detective in spirit who came to visit with his wife.

"I'm hearing a *bang* and seeing a bedroom," I told his wife.

"Yes, he shot himself in the head in our bedroom," she acknowledged as she covered her face with her hands.

"Your love . . . He feels your love now but thought you were going to leave him."

"Yes," she whispered. "He never thought I would stay."

At that point, I smelled alcohol and felt a fuzzy feeling in my head, which indicates that a spirit struggled with alcohol and drug addiction while on Earth.

"He was an alcoholic and struggled with drug addiction, yes?"

"Yes," she whispered again, in agreement.

Suddenly a feeling of deep remorse and pain washed over me, and I heard the words, "I'm sorry," which I repeated for his wife.

"I know, honey," she gently said, and I knew that she was speaking directly to the man she loved.

"I will never leave you," her husband added.

"That's what I need to hear. I thought that by choosing to die, you were leaving me," she replied.

Once again, I felt the pain of remorse. At that moment, I had no doubt that this man, who had been afraid of abandonment, understood fully the pain he had caused by choosing to die.

As a medium, and also as Tommy's cousin, there is one thing that I have found most difficult to understand: those who choose suicide often do not realize the impact that their death will have on those left behind. Spirits who have died by suicide have said things to me like, "I thought my family would be better off without me," and it's challenging for me to imagine that they really believed that their family and friends wouldn't miss them.

Some spirits are matter of fact about choosing suicide. More than once, a spirit has said to me, "I was done." In other cases, those who pass by suicide have no idea how much they were loved until after they've passed. Loving someone, despite their choice to die, is perhaps the greatest way to experience and express unconditional love.

To understand what happens to people who commit suicide, it might be helpful to share an actual conversation with someone who committed suicide.

Early on a Friday evening, I opened the door to my office reception area, where an athletic-looking couple was waiting. Chandra and Cal entered my office, and we joked about the swallow-up sofa along one wall, which, although comfortable, is difficult to get out of once you're sitting in it.

After opening with my usual blessing, I noticed a young male in spirit in the room. An older man in spirit also caught my eye as he strode across the room authoritatively and stood directly behind Cal. This spirit gave me the feeling of a father and stood there silently, with his arms crossed. Then he saluted; and behind him, I saw ships, water, and men in Navy uniforms. I heard the names Rudy, Norman, and Michael—all names that were acknowledged as accurate by Cal: Rudy was his father's middle name, and he had been in the Merchant Marine; his grandfather, Norman, had been in the Navy; and Michael, Cal's son, had died most recently.

The father (Rudy) gave me the sense that he was a hardworking, upstanding man who didn't believe in mediumship or metaphysics in general while he was on Earth, but he had a reason to overcome his prejudice to speak with me: he wanted Cal to know that he was with his grandson.

"I asked my dad to take care of our son, Michael," Cal confirmed after clearing his throat.

Before I could get more information about that, Michael stood next to Chandra.

"I have the sensation that my head is being tapped on, so I think that he died with an injury to the head. I don't feel pain . . . or fear.

This happened too quickly for pain to register in the body. I'm hearing a gunshot," I relayed to Chandra.

"Yes, I understand," she said. "Our son shot himself in the head."

Interestingly enough, her son hadn't said the word *suicide*. This might seem surprising, since cause of death is a valuable piece of evidence for sitters; however, in my experience, those who die from suicide sometimes avoid saying so. It is almost as though the word itself is too loaded and painful a reminder for those left behind. In other cases, spirits give me the word *suicide* so dispassionately that it seems as though they are referring to a third party, not themselves. In truth, I don't know if a spirit chooses to mention suicide or not in their message in order to protect their loved ones, or whether their healing after death releases them from identifying with the action of suicide.

Michael tapped my left shoulder and I heard "chip."

"Michael had a chip on his shoulder—he was angry and didn't feel as though he belonged," I stated as he gave me a sense of deep loneliness.

"I would say that this is indeed true," Cal agreed.

"He gives me the feeling of a broken heart; a relationship with a girl ended shortly before he died," I added, and Chandra acknowledged that to be accurate.

Information was relayed to me without emotion; no hurt appeared to linger. I heard "no blame" and saw a vision of breadcrumbs on the ground.

"He is showing me breadcrumbs, the bits of his life that led him toward his death; it was the anger—that chip on his shoulder—that placed those crumbs at his feet."

Next to Michael, an older female, giving me the feeling of a grandmother, appeared suddenly. The name Bertha popped into my mind.

"That's my mother's name!" exclaimed Cal.

How odd, I thought. Bertha was standing near her daughter-in-law, Chandra, rather than her own son. Then I realized that she was aligning herself with her grandson.

"She loves this boy!" I exclaimed. It felt as though my heart was expanding with love beyond its capacity to contain it.

"Oh yes, Bertha *loved* Michael. They were very close," Chandra confirmed.

At that moment, Michael wrote "no escape" in the air between us. I knew that he was making clear that suicide didn't allow him to escape his life and his choices.

You see, when we die, we experience our lives from the perspectives of everyone we've loved and everyone we've wounded. Sometimes, those we wound deepest are those we love most. But love like the love that Bertha dropped into my heart allows us to face *anything*. Love makes looking at even the most painful of things a bearable and even healing experience.

Michael took me suddenly to the time of his birth. He gave me a feeling in my chest—a medical issue.

"Yes," his mother said. "Not a big problem, but he had to be suctioned."

Her son gave me the sense that he could have opted out of life at that point but decided to stay. "I wanted to be born to you," he told his mother.

Before Michael's statement could be fully appreciated, my attention was drawn to Bertha. (Communication can move quickly from spirit to spirit). Bertha showed me a kitchen and mentioned the name Eleanor.

"Eleanor was her sister," Cal interjected.

"Well, she apparently liked to cook," I added.

Chandra laughed and said that her son used to say that she had cooked him up in a pan—a family joke that underscored his sense that he really didn't belong in the family. In retrospect, not a very funny joke.

At that moment, I saw Cal's father and the grandfather named Norman standing behind him. Michael joined the lineup, and I heard in my ear, "I don't have a chip on my shoulder anymore; I'm a chip off the old block." This young man in spirit used an old-fashioned saying to indicate that he now identifies completely with being a member of the family. Four generations of fathers and sons stood together.

Michael then appeared next to Chandra and gave me a feeling of intense love and peace surrounding the two of them. "Your son gives me the sense that you have made peace with his death. No matter what, you love him anyway."

"Yes, that's true," she agreed. "I will always love him." And that declaration ended the session.

Although this encounter with a young man who died by suicide doesn't necessarily represent all who die by suicide, it does illustrate salient points about the impact of suicide on the soul.

There is a common idea that when we die, there is a life review—a *Life's Greatest Hits* album or a highlight reel. After communicating with thousands of spirits, I've learned that this isn't exactly true. Yes, there is a life review, but it is a full-impact, fully immersive situation. Here on Earth, we're told to "walk a mile in someone else's shoes"; ironically, it is in the afterlife, where, as spirits, we don't even need shoes, that we can actually experience life from another person's perspective.

The good news? As difficult as this may sound, the experience of unconditional love leads to understanding, not punishment, even though we may not have acknowledged the harm we caused while living on Earth. This is one of the reasons why, I think, a thematic refrain of personal responsibility is so prevalent in messages that spirits give me to share; "he made me do it" isn't a justification in the afterlife. At the frequency of love, every spirit acknowledges his or her part in whether love was expressed on the planet or not. And this includes self-love.

In my first book, *I'm Not Dead, I'm Different*, I devoted an entire chapter to suicide. The subject affects me deeply and personally because of the death of my cousin Tommy. Perhaps this connection is the reason that much of my work as a medium is to allow spirits to answer the painful questions their suicide has left unanswered. Frequently, I've been stunned by groups of spirits who died by suicide and attend group events—as a group—with their loved ones. For example, at an event in Laguna Beach, spirits stood behind loved ones in the back row, and they all had committed suicide. In that situation, I simply spoke with one after another, right down the row. The people sitting in that row hadn't all come to the event together, so they were astonished to discover how much they had in common.

So, what happens to people who commit suicide? The same thing that happens to anyone who dies: other spirits welcome, love, and help them experience and face their pain and the pain they have caused others. Dying from suicide or dying from cancer doesn't come with tickets to different places in the afterlife—one way of dying isn't more spiritually acceptable than another. And *no* way of dying separates us from love.

> *For more on how spirits view suicide, read Q&A number 55, "Do spirits agree with us about what is good and what is bad"? in chapter 9, "The Big Questions."*

22. Is it true that you can't take anything with you when you die?

When people say, "You can't take it with you," it is more often than not a rationale for spending every last penny on whatever might be at hand. So, the answer to this question seems obvious, doesn't it? Well, maybe not. In actuality, there's plenty that we can take with us when we die!

A young woman in spirit—while visiting with me and her mother and sister—outlined in wonderful detail the things she was and was not able to pack in her heavenly luggage. The mother, Angela (an elegant, petite woman with enviably coiffed hair), and sister, Kathy (petite, athletic, and energetic), sat side by side on the couch in my office. Annalise, a beautiful young woman in spirit with long, silky blond hair, stood between them with a dog—a lab mix—by her side.

"That's the dog we had when we were kids!" Kathy exclaimed.

At that moment, the spirit shifted her appearance and became a dark-haired little girl.

"Yes, she had dark hair when she was small," Angela confirmed.

"She just yelled 'Surprise!' at me, and I have the sense that she is referring to her birth. She wasn't expected, right?" I asked.

"Yes, that's right," Angela confirmed.

"Oh, and she gives me a sense that there was a concern around her birth—she almost died while being born. Feels like a breach," I added.

"Yes, we nearly lost her before she was even born," Angela said, tears in her eyes.

For a moment, the four of us sat with the memory of a surprise pregnancy, a breach, and a dark-haired girl with her dog. The joy of the birth and the happiness of childhood were palpable to all of us.

In that moment, Annalise demonstrated that memory is one thing that spirits take with them from their time on Earth. These memories include what has happened very early in life, even during the birth process. Spirits also share memories of what has occurred during times where the brain has been incapacitated, even if it seems as though consciousness is severely impaired or nonexistent.

As I continued my time with Annalise and her family, she showed me herself surrounded by dogs and horses. I described the animals, and her sister and mother recognized some but not all. I heard the word *rescue* in my ear.

"Oh yes, she was big into animal rescue," Kathy said.

"Well, she apparently still is!" I replied. "In fact, you're looking for another dog, right?"

"Y-y-yes," Kathy replied, somewhat hesitantly.

"She's still working with animal rescue, so don't worry. You won't have to go out looking—a dog is coming your way! Your sister wants to be sure that every homeless animal finds a loving home."

"Annalise used to say that exact thing when she was here—she wanted to spend her life helping animals find loving homes," Kathy added.

By iterating her life's desire, Annalise made it clear that another thing we take with us when we die is the essence of who we are. Annalise is a loving, caring spirit just as she was a loving, caring person in life. Character qualities such as compassion, joy, sincerity, loyalty, honesty, and trustworthiness are eternal; and unlike our physicality we take these attributes with us when we leave the body behind.

Annalise switched gears smoothly and moved swiftly from the subject of rescued pets to cars and her sister's career.

"Annalise is showing me a car—you talk with her while driving, correct?" I asked Kathy.

"Yes, but I wasn't sure she was always listening."

"You've been talking with her about your work, a new career move."

"Yes, that's right."

"Annalise gives me the feeling that you are at the point of making a choice between several options."

"Yes, I am."

"You are or will be asked about a proposal, which includes your fee."

"Yes, I was asked by a company to consult, but I'm not sure what I should charge."

"Annalise says, 'Know your worth. Now is the time to appreciate what you bring to the athletic world and the work world. Know. Your. Worth.'"

"That's always been a challenge for me," Kathy acknowledged. "Annalise always had such faith in me."

Kathy started to grin wider and wider as she realized that her sister was completing what she thought had been only a one-sided conversation. "Dying doesn't end the conversation or our connections," I said, stating the obvious.

Annalise had added another item to our list of things that we can take with us when we die—our connections. Spirits remain in contact with us and are interested in our lives. Even though we may doubt or question it at times, those we love in spirit are present, supporting and guiding us.

After that exchange with her sister, Annalise turned my attention toward her mother.

She drew a big heart around her mother that completely engulfed her. I felt an expanding of love in my heart. "Annalise is showing me that you are surrounded by love," I told her. Angela stayed silent as tears slid down her cheeks.

I then saw the heart expanding to include Annalise, her mother, and her sister. It was like a giant Valentine's Day box of humans.

"Annalise has placed all of you in this love *together*. She died feeling loved, and she still feels loved by both of you. And she loves you both in return." (Even *I* felt loved, and I was sitting outside the love box!)

In that graphic and dramatic way, Annalise demonstrated that another thing we take with us when we die—and maybe the most important thing—is love. Death doesn't diminish love; and in many cases, death expands love and makes it more accessible.

So, if anyone says, "You can't take it with you," remember that the aphorism isn't true when it comes to memory, essence, connection, and most of all, *love*.

23. Is there a waiting period before spirits can be contacted?

When I began working as a medium about twenty-five years ago, it was commonly accepted that spirits would not communicate immediately upon passing. It became standard to suggest a waiting period of six months or so as the spirit recovered energy lost during illness at the end of life or learned how to communicate from the afterlife.

That belief is now being called into question, sometimes in spectacular ways. For example, at an event not long ago in California, a young man in spirit appeared to give a message to one of his high school teachers in the audience. The young man had only gone missing the night before, his body not yet found.

This was indeed a dramatic moment at the event, but spirits don't employ drama to entertain us; they use it to get our attention. In this case, there was nearly no time between this young man's disappearance, his death, and his appearance at an event. This was highly unusual and therefore a fact worth noting. Although surprised at the young man's appearance, I was willing to let it be instructive rather than unsettling. What this young man in spirit didn't share with me was how he died. I'm curious by nature, but I've learned to let spirits provide the information necessary for their purposes.

Before events, I always ask the spirits to teach me something new. Consequently, I pay attention when I have a spirit encounter that is unusual in some way. This visit raised questions such as: Could this young man be demonstrating a "reset" of the time frame between death and connection? And why come to this particular event to meet with his teacher?

Upon reflection, the first thing that occurred to me was that, while those close to him were traumatized by his disappearance, the spirit connected *immediately* with someone who was removed from his *inner* circle. Spirits are opportunists; and this young man in spirit knew that someone in his network of family, friends, and acquaintances was going to be in the presence of a medium. This was one of the first experiences of many that prompted me to consider that a delay in communication wasn't from the spirit side at all. Could it be that grief, grievance, trauma, and emotional upset on the Earth side might be greater factors in disrupting communication than previously thought?

As a medium, I'm in contact with many people whose lives have changed (often suddenly and drastically) on a particular day at a particular time. I often hear this statement from sitters: "From that moment, my life was never the same." The accessibility to mediums isn't the only option that spirits use to make themselves known immediately or soon after dying. As acceptance and understanding of spirit communication has grown, so have reports of direct communications from loved ones in spirit.

This point is underscored by the experience of a grieving sister who told me about the night her brother died: she was awakened by his voice calling her name, and shortly after that, her phone rang—it was her sister calling about their brother's death.

The trauma and high emotions surrounding the death of a loved one may make it difficult to perceive the spirit's presence. That was the case in the death of an athletic, energetic young man who was and still is devoted to his mother, Carol. During our session, he told me that he and his mom had spoken by phone right before he died. Carol acknowledged that her son had called her twenty minutes before he was to arrive at her house. As time went by and he didn't arrive, however, she assumed he had made a stop on the way. But then the police knocked at her door; it was to let her know that her son had swerved off the road, hit a pole, and died instantly. The young man in spirit had shared the details of this horrific moment to let his mother know that, in spirit, he had been standing right beside her. After she spoke with the police, he tried to hold her up as she fell to the ground in shock.

As suddenly as this son's physical life ended, he was at his mother's side to comfort her and continue their relationship. She, of course, was only seeing the ending at that moment; he, on the other hand, was offering a beginning.

Spirits know that life doesn't end with death. And now, because we are willing to accept their presence, even while grieving, spirits are demonstrating to mediums—and in fact, *all* of us—that no time is needed between their death and the continuation of their relationships with loved ones, albeit in a new way.

So why the change? I think that there is a twofold reason for this: first, in years past, the energy of spirits (and mediums) was directed toward raising interest and acceptance of spirit communication; and second, when a medium didn't make a connection with the spirit, it was assumed that the spirit needed to adjust to the afterlife.

For spirits, there is no gap between living, dying, and living again; and they want us to know this too. There doesn't need to be a gap between our last conversation with them on Earth and our next one with them in spirit. That said, they understand that we might be the ones who need time. But don't worry; whenever we're ready, they'll be there.

4

Life in the Afterlife

24. Do spirits need to learn how to connect with us, in the physical realm?

Yes, they do.

Imagine if, suddenly, you were unable to speak or use hand gestures to drive a point home or move objects with ease. After a life in a physical body, spirits live in a world of expanded consciousness, thought, and energy. As a medium, it is my job to be aware of the subtle communications from the spirits as their energy interacts with mine. It has also been my experience that spirits, who are new to the afterlife, need to be coached by more experienced spirits, who are good communicators and act as my guides.

Over the years, I've developed a lexicon of symbols and other shortcuts to make it easier for us (the spirits and I) to understand one another. Sometimes I can almost hear my guides saying to a spirit, "If you show her this or that, she'll get it." For instance, there are times when I can feel the spirits touching my body playfully (children in spirit seem to do this with great frequency); and when I feel my energy centers being tickled, it is almost as though the spirit is asking, "Can you feel this? Can you feel that? Huh? *Huh???*" I'm even willing to undergo a bit of practice prodding so that a spirit can use his or her new skills to touch a loved one's hair or give a heavenly kiss on the cheek.

What has surprised me is the growing number of people who want to learn how to communicate like a spirit *before* they die! As the "right to die" movement resulted in legislation, I began to be contacted by people who were wrapping up their lives on Earth with medically assisted suicide.

Marisol was one such person; she had heard about my work from one of my clients. My assistant set up a time for us to speak by phone several days before she was scheduled to die.

Prior to the call, I meditated as I do before any session. When the phone rang, I answered the call with "Hello. This is Hollister Rand." In response, I heard a cheery and energetic voice say, "Hi, I'm ending my life and want to know how I can best communicate with people on Earth once I'm on the other side."

I laughed, which might seem inappropriate, but this woman's matter-of-fact, get-to-the-point request was charming—I liked her immediately. Fortunately, she laughed as well. We were off to a good start!

"I would assume that you want to assure the people you love on Earth that you will continue to be with them and support them in life—that death isn't the end of your relationship," I offered.

"Yes, absolutely!" she responded enthusiastically. "I want to continue to help my family, and I want them to be absolutely sure that I'm always backing them up!"

"You've already done most of the work by setting your intention," I informed her. "But I would caution you against presetting the exact way that you will make yourself known."

"Really?" she questioned with surprise. Marisol certainly wouldn't have been the first person hoping to create a code word or predetermine a series of actions to convince loved ones that, "Hey, it's really me!"

"Communication from the other side isn't a cloak-and-dagger deal with codes and synchronized watches," I told her. "I've discovered over the years that the most effective spirit communication is the result of anticipation that a connection will be made without the expectation that messages will appear in a specific way."

I went on to explain to Marisol that expectation constricts the energy required for connection, because an expectation is nothing other than an implicit demand that things go a certain way. Here's an analogy that may help to make the concept clear.

When I attended a J.Lo concert at T-Mobile Arena in Las Vegas, there was only one way in (through security) and one way out. Naturally, the more than 17,000 people attending created a logjam at the exit; spirit communication is like that. All of the fantastic bits of evidence that spirits can provide to establish their identity can't find their way out because there is only one exit door. However, when spirit communication is approached in an open, accepting way, the energy flows freely, with plenty of entrances and exits for the information. This allows spirits a lot of latitude for providing bountiful evidence on their own terms, in their own way.

To encourage Marisol further that her messages would reach loved ones, I added, "Also, you'll have plenty of people in your spirit network of family and friends to help you get your point across to those living on Earth. Communication is a group effort, not a one-woman show."

"Huh," she said and then paused. "So, I guess I have to get my ego out of the way?"

I laughed again. (Who knew that talking about death could be so much fun?)

"Oh, your ego won't be a problem; like any other thing required for navigating through life on the Earth plane, it drops away at the higher frequencies of love. Think of it this way: the ego is the appendix of the afterlife—not necessary and easily removed if toxic."

She laughed again and mentioned that her family wanted her to have a traditional funeral after her death.

"Well, you know that's for them, right?" I interjected.

"Yeah, I know they need it. But there's a bit of a problem, because my friends who are Buddhists want my body to lie in the house for three days while they pray. My family doesn't want that to happen. They're really uncomfortable with that idea."

"Don't worry," I told her. "Your Buddhist friends can pray for you regardless—their prayers and those of others can really lift your spirit to the higher frequencies of love, peace, and joy."

"Good, good," she responded thoughtfully.

I could tell that there was something else troubling her, so I waited.

"My family members are born-again Christians, and they want me to accept Jesus as my Savior before I die. I was raised a Christian Scientist, and Jesus and I are on good terms, I think—I like Jesus. What do you think?"

Finally, we were at the crux of the matter. Maybe she wanted to know whether after she died, she could communicate proof that either Jesus or Buddha was right! However, at that moment, I was inspired by spirits to look beyond disparate religious beliefs. I noticed that Marisol's true concern was how she could honor all the religious traditions of her family and friends, each of whom wanted to ensure her the best dying experience.

In response to the unvoiced question, I answered, "Spirits of different religions talk to me about living at the divine frequencies of love, joy, and peace. Religion may be the doorway, but the destination is the same. In your case, the Buddhist and Christian doors are wide open, so don't worry; you cannot end up in a place that sets you apart from those you love."

There was silence on the other end of the phone.

I added, "It seems to me that you are very concerned about taking care of your friends and family and making sure that they are okay with your death. Am I right about that?"

Marisol acknowledged that this was the case.

"And they are obviously very concerned about you as well. You're all expressing love to one another; and in the end, *that* is the conduit of communication between both sides of life."

There was such a lengthy silence that I thought the call might have been dropped. Then I heard a sigh, which sounded like relief. Marisol finally said, "Thank you for your time. I really appreciated your answers to my questions."

"I'm very glad that we had time together as well. Hope to talk with you again," I said, rather absentmindedly, and then added—"perhaps from the other side." She laughed, as did I, and we ended our talk about death with a shared smile.

After I hung up the phone, I sat quietly, thinking about the conversation with Marisol, who had only a short time to live.

It occurred to me that although most of us won't know the exact day and hour of our passing like Marisol, we can still prepare. Giving and receiving love on the Earth plane keeps the love lines open and functional, and facilitates communication when we're no longer in a body. Living in love is what each of us can do to help awaken the world to what's *really* important.

So Marisol, cheers! I'm looking forward to talking with you again soon.

25. Are there seasons/climates in the afterlife?

When spirits show me glimpses of the afterlife, the weather often reflects their favorite season. For example, during a session with his mother, a young man in spirit who loved snowboarding appeared in skiwear, with a snowy mountain in the background. Spirits show me favorite spring flowers, fall colors, beach scenes—whatever natural landscapes inspired them during their time on Earth.

When I connect with several spirits during the same session, they each may describe a different season. Here on the Earth plane, we must physically move to a new location to get the weather we desire (which is why I live in Los Angeles for most of the year rather than New York). For spirits, however, seasons in the afterlife are more of a state of mind than a force of nature.

That being said, loved ones in spirit may use the seasons of *our* world to make themselves known. To help you understand how this may be, I've put together a list of some of the ways spirits have used typical spring things (for instance) to communicate with us on Earth.

Spring Break

"Your father gives me a Florida connection with your son and a fraternity," I told a lady at a spirit circle.

"Of course he does," she replied. "My son's on spring break in Miami with his fraternity brothers."

As the message continued, it became clear that not only was her beloved father protecting his grandson during the craziness of spring break, he was also joining in the festivities himself—and having a great time! Grandfather and grandson were buddies here on Earth, and death had not changed that relationship.

How nice to know that our young are looked after while stepping beyond their parents' reach. However, when tragedy strikes, it may seem as though spirits have fallen down on the job. I remember a session in which a young woman with great promise mentioned dying in a van accident during a spring-break island getaway.

"Grandma Ellen was right there with me," said the young woman to her mother in the sitting. And her mother wept as she replied, "My only hope in this situation was that my mother met my daughter when she passed. I was so afraid that she'd be alone."

We need never fear for those we love—or for ourselves. But rest assured: we—and they—are never alone.

Spring Cleaning

"Your mother, Isabel, is here in spirit and putting boxes at your feet," I mentioned to a sitter during a phone session. "She's helping you with spring cleaning. She wants you to know that it is okay to donate the things that she can't use any longer."

There was silence on the phone line.

With a catch in her voice, the sitter said, "Before this appointment, I asked Mom to let me know if it is okay to give her things away to people who need them."

At a spirit circle in a private home, a father in spirit reminded his daughter of the undergrowth around the house that needed to be cleaned out in the spring (she and her husband had helped with that chore each year). As her father continued to remind them of spring chores, he also mentioned that he liked to be in the backyard by the fountain. At that moment, the family dog ran to the doors leading out to the backyard and began to bark. I don't think any of us in that room doubted that this usually quiet dog was seeing a father in spirit enjoying a spring day in his favorite spot.

Birds and Other Winged Creatures

"Your mom loves hummingbirds," I told two sisters during a phone session. "She sits on the back deck and invites them to visit. In fact, she's letting me know that you just put up another feeder in her honor."

"I did that this morning!" one of the daughters exclaimed.

I have heard many times from spirits that they will let loved ones know that they're around by inspiring birds to appear. Hawks and owls swooping by, feathers materializing from apparently nowhere, dragonflies and butterflies brightening grief-filled moments, and hummingbirds buzzing in front of faces are often hellos from loved ones in spirit.

Sea Creatures

Although there seems to be a natural affinity between winged creatures and the spirits, sea creatures such as whales, turtles, and sea lions are also favorites. However, spirits will enlist unusual animals to draw attention to their presence as well. Brandy, a sixteen-year-old in spirit, provided the perfect example of such an unusual animal encounter.

While growing up, Brandy loved going to Florida with her family. (She established this fact by projecting a map of the state onto the screen of my mind.) Immediately after providing that clear piece of information, Brandy showed me a picture that was ridiculous and confusing—a vision of swimming cows. With no further explanation provided by Brandy, I turned to Elaine, her mother, and said, "Brandy is showing me cows swimming in what looks like the sea."

Elaine looked shocked and sat back on the sofa. After reaching for a tissue, she explained.

"During one of our family trips, we took the kids to see manatees. Brandy announced to us that she wanted to spend her life with manatees, and we discussed the possibility of her studying to become a marine biologist."

Do you know what a manatee is? Have you seen one? If not, you aren't alone. I'm familiar with them because of spending extensive time in Florida. Their nickname—sea cows—is apt because they are large, plant-eating, peaceful mammals.

Toward the end of the time with her mother, Brandy gave me the date March 17. I assumed that she was indicating that St. Patrick's Day was important to the family, but that wasn't the case.

"It was on March 17 last year that our entire extended family celebrated Brandy's life in Florida. While we stood near the water, a large group of manatees gathered. I'd never seen anything like it!" Elaine exclaimed.

I have no doubt that Brandy, the girl who loved manatees, is loved by them in return. This unusual gathering of sea cows was, in my opinion, a sure sign that Brandy was present for her celebration of life.

Wind Chimes

Ah, the sound of wind chimes from a gentle spring breeze . . . As I discovered from speaking to Omer, a young man in spirit, he could make chimes ring even without a breeze! His mother confirmed that chimes hanging in her son's room started to ring during the night. When she got up to investigate, she could see the chimes swaying even though no windows were open and no fans were blowing. Omer loved wind chimes from the time he was a baby; even in spirit, he still loves wind chimes, and uses them to let his mother know that he is around.

Gardens

Spirits speak about gardens (and flowers) *a lot*. During one session, a mother in spirit showed herself surrounded by a magnificent garden. As she beamed in the midst of it, she said, "No weeding needed."

Spirits may show me a specific flower—a rose, daisy, lily, or iris, for example—that was either a favorite or shares their name. Vegetable and herb gardens are also a topic of conversation for spirits, often because gardens represent a person's determination to take care of themselves and their families while on Earth as well as in spirit.

Recently, however, I spoke with a grandfather in spirit who spoke about gardens in a different way.

"Your grandfather is gardening," I told his granddaughter.

"He loved his garden," she confirmed.

"Your grandfather is letting me know that he is planting your dreams in his garden so that they can grow. He is tending to your wishes and your intentions so that they can become real for you here on Earth."

We were both struck by the beauty of that statement. Just the idea that those we love in spirit can help our dreams to grow—that spirits can help to cocreate our reality—has prompted me into considering spring planting in a more expansive way. That grandfather's message was a wow moment for me.

It isn't only spring that spirits share with us—all seasons are celebrated. And loved ones in spirit can help to make holidays memorable as well.

> *For more on celebrating the holidays with loved ones in spirit, read chapter 8, "Spirited Occasions."*

26. Do spirits have jobs?

In the afterlife, there are no mortgages, taxes, or budgets to manage. That doesn't mean, however, that spirits loaf around floating on clouds. After years of communicating with them, I've come to the conclusion that nothing happens on Earth without a contributing spirit component.

When a client's husband appeared for a visit, it wasn't just to express love to his wife; he wanted to assure her that he was keeping busy by instructing his protégé, a young woman he had hired shortly before he died.

"My husband was a workaholic," his wife said with a smile. "It figures that even death wouldn't stop him from going to the office."

I don't know whether this man's protégé knew she was being "instructed," though guidance from spirits can be quite obvious—when you know how to look for it. For example, in a situation in which a daughter was taking over her father's business, books with essential information actually fell off the shelf at her feet when she visited the bookstore!

In another instance, when a loving wife came for a session, her husband in spirit mentioned that he was guiding purchases for an art foundation in his name. She was delighted. "That was his baby," she told me. "I knew his love of art wouldn't die with him." Later in the year, I received a phone message from this woman, who said that a small private collection of one of her husband's favorite artists had become available. Rather than putting the collection up for auction, the seller allowed the foundation to purchase it at a set price. She heard through the grapevine that the seller just "knew" that his art would be appreciated, valued, and loved through the work of the foundation. These synchronicities clearly have the "fingerprints" of spirits on them!

Let me say again that it is my personal belief that nothing happens here on Earth without the influence of spirits as part of the mix. Our thoughts, intentions, and desires—all of which have an energetic "handprint"—can align with the energetic match for those of spirits. In the case of the art foundation, a love for art and a particular artist set up a link of energy between a spirit, a person, and an artist, drawing these people in a shared direction (although, with free will, there's always the choice to disagree with the direction of that pull!). In essence, humans and spirits can shake hands on a deal or walk away from it.

I have also experienced cases when a spirit "expert" assists those on Earth. This was never truer than with a budding performer who attended a spirit circle. As I looked behind the sitter, I saw Woody Guthrie, the American singer-songwriter famously known for writing the song "This Land Is Your Land." (Fortunately, my mother was a fan of folk music, so I recognized him.) Next to Woody was a large grassy area with a stage, and I was hearing his music being sung by a female voice. When I reported what I was seeing and hearing to the sitter, her eyes widened. After taking a deep breath, she volunteered that she was performing a retrospective of Woody Guthrie songs at an outdoor music festival. It was to be her first time in front of an audience of that size. Some may think that this vision was a premonition, but that's not the case. When we think, create, and work toward a goal, from the spirits' perspective it is as though the goals are reached and the work completed.

Woody's appearance could have been interpreted a number of ways. However, my "shorthand" with spirits includes a link between where a person stands, who they are to the sitter, and their purpose in appearing. In this situation, Woody was standing directly behind the sitter, which indicated to me that he was backing her up while she stepped out into the public eye.

It might seem odd that a music icon would help a musician he didn't know personally; in actuality, this is a good example of how spirits help humankind. Spirits use their expertise learned on Earth to inspire and teach people in their field. It is stunning to consider that scientists may make breakthroughs not only based on their own discoveries but also with the assistance from researchers who have died!

Fantastical as it sounds, I've had experiences that support this idea. For example, at a group event, I saw Nobel Prize–winning physicist Niels Bohr standing next to a young man in the audience. The Danish physicist (yes, I love folk music *and* physics) gave me the sense that he was helping the young man with his work. Imagine my surprise—and the surprise of others in the group—when the young man announced that not only was he a physics major, he was also writing a paper about where Niels Bohr's work could lead.

Much of our time on Earth is spent preparing for work, looking for it, and then looking forward to retiring from it. Well, guess what? Spirits don't have a retirement plan! As long as there is work to be done in the world, they'll pitch in. And you'll know when spirits are pitching in when a solution presents itself and your immediate response is, "What are the odds?" For instance, when I was hoping to find a mini, well-behaved, non-barking rescue Chihuahua who could help provide comfort for people in grief, I was told that it was an impossible task. Well, a woman at a spirit circle sent me a photo of a three-pound Chihuahua up for adoption. Imagine my surprise when I discovered that the rescue organization was run by a dear friend's sister! I had even done events for the rescue's volunteers.

When I was ready to adopt a second dog (could lightning strike twice?), spirits gave me an extra nudge. One night, while I was out of town, I heard in my head: *Search small-animal rescue.* I did so and up popped a photo of a 2.8-pound Chihuahua. My application was approved within hours, and the foster home was less than twenty minutes from my hotel. Bodhi and the new dog hit it off; and that's how Amara came to me. Two mini, well-behaved, silent, rescue Chihuahuas. What are the odds?

Take a moment to think about your own work life. Do you feel called to a different type of work? Are you looking to start a business? Are you preparing for a future career and are unsure which certificate program is best to pursue? Don't worry. Spirits—even those you don't know personally—will pitch in and help guide you. As my mother used to say, "Many hands make light work." I think *all* spirits, not only the loved ones that we know, would agree with that statement—in *every* sense.

27. Do spirits go on vacation?

Actually . . . yes, they do. But probably not in the way you may think.

Spirits travel (sometimes extensively) and often to places they wanted to visit while living on Earth. (So keep adding to your bucket list!) Spirits have told me about expeditions to Mount Everest, safaris to Africa, journeys to Stonehenge, and surfing trips to Hawaii—all experienced *after* they died!

One young man in spirit told his sister (through me) that he was with her when she climbed Machu Picchu. He showed me a picture in my mind of a red bandana and a photo of himself. His sister confirmed that she had worn his bandana and carried his photo during the trip. She and her brother had talked about going to Peru together, but he died before they made any concrete plans. She hoped that by bringing his favorite bandana, he would be along on the journey. Well, he *was*!

In another session, a son in spirit reminded his mother of their summers by the lake. In this way, he was making it clear to her that although death had separated him from his physical body, it didn't rob him of his memories. When that same son in spirit mentioned the family reunion planned for July, he made it clear that he is also aware of what is happening in the family currently. He then went on to mention that he would show up in the family photos to "prove" that he was present. (One of the ways that spirits demonstrate their presence is to show up as orbs, mist, or streaks of light in photos.)

As you plan a summer getaway, or think about vacations past, please know that those you love in spirit share in your memories and will join you on cruises, in tents, at the beach, at the zoo, by the pool, at the top of a mountain, or even as you sit quietly in your home on a staycation. For spirits, a vacation isn't an opportunity to escape from the routine of eternity but an opportunity to inspire laughter and memories, and to join in new experiences with those they love.

28. Do spirits have to eat?

Spirits don't have physical bodies and, therefore, don't need the nutrients provided by breakfast, lunch, and dinner. So, in short, the answer to this question is no. But that doesn't stop spirits from talking about food!

I used to think that spirits talked to me about food because of my personal obsession with it. (My bedtime reading consists of the latest cookbook.) Fortunately, the food thing isn't all about me! When a friend met with a well-known medium to hear from her husband, the medium referred repeatedly to her husband's devotion to barbecuing. My friend, hoping to hear how much her husband loved *her*, was irritated, to say the least.

Food doesn't just nourish our bodies; few of us eat solely for physical survival. Food is a major concern, regardless of whether there is too much of it or too little. A considerable amount of time is spent talking about food, preparing food, and working so we can buy food. What would a birthday celebration be without a cake?

Speaking of cake, a son in spirit asked his mother to bake his favorite cake for his birthday (German chocolate, by the way), but it wasn't because his spirit needed the calories. Instead, the request assured his mother that he remembers her expressions of love and can still join in the celebration of his life.

When a great-uncle who'd died of starvation in a concentration camp talked to me about the afterlife having tables laden with food, he was speaking of the abundance he found in spirit that he had found lacking on Earth. Although spirits don't actually eat the food, they enjoy the memory of taste and can create a gorgeous dinner, much as an artist paints a still life of a fall harvest from memory.

When a young woman who'd passed from complications due to anorexia shared with me that she is enjoying food and can finally see herself as she really is, her parents knew that she was free of her affliction. (Spirits enjoy food by remembering the taste of it.) Another young woman in spirit who'd obsessed about watching her weight while on Earth told me, "I can eat whatever I want here!" (Food in thought and in memory has no calories!) So you see, everyone has his or her own idea of what makes the afterlife heavenly. (My afterlife will be full of ice cream [Ben & Jerry's, not low-calorie Halo Top] and candy [Belgium chocolate, in particular].)

When a mother in spirit mentioned preparing Thanksgiving dinner for those who had recently died, she was demonstrating the welcoming nature for which she was known on earth. (Her son confirmed that at Thanksgiving, his mother always invited people who had no family or were new to the neighborhood.)

When those we love in spirit share their likes and dislikes of particular foods, these characteristics identify them as clearly as fingerprints would. One father in spirit reminded his son of a particular ice-cream vendor (by name) in a town (he also gave me the name) where they would go on Sundays to get pistachio ice cream and hot fudge. This memory was so personal and specific that the son had no doubt that his father was speaking with me, a medium.

Spirits can also impress us (especially those of us who are sensitive to them) to eat at a particular restaurant or to eat food that is normally not preferred. These impressions may come in several different ways, including our sense of taste and smell. A mother with a son in spirit smells pizza every now and then when she isn't near a Domino's or Little Caesars. When that happens, she'll contact a few of her son's friends and have a pizza party. Oddly enough, these spontaneous pizza parties coincide with a friend's birthday or other significant occasion. Spirits may also use an energy pull, usually from the solar plexus (the midsection of the body), to draw our attention to a restaurant serving their favorite cuisine. This happened to me in Huntington Beach, California.

Before starting a day of sittings, I was drawn to a German deli near where I was staying; I felt excitement at the very thought of eating breakfast there. Before I knew it, my plate was piled high with all sorts of meats (with names I couldn't pronounce) and extremely rich pastries. *Why am I eating all this?* I asked myself, thoroughly annoyed that I would then have to diet for a week.

During the first session of the day, a man in spirit came to visit with a lovely lady, his widow. After identifying himself as her husband George, I told her that I was hearing German in my ear. "Of course you are," she said. "My husband was German." And then I got it. That big German breakfast I ordered that morning? George sent me to that deli! George's widow confirmed that he enjoyed a large breakfast each and every morning, and especially liked the pastries. Fabulous. The last thing I need is to eat for spirits too!

Food is important to us on Earth and to our loved ones in spirit. Food is about family. Food is about memories. And most of all, food is an expression of love, of sustenance, and of abundance on this side and the other side of life.

29. Do soldiers in spirit talk about combat and its effect on them and their families?

I've spoken to soldiers in spirit from American wars, including the War of Independence, the Civil War, the Vietnam War, and those fighting in our current conflicts around the world. In addition, I've communicated with servicemen and -women who have been on opposing sides.

During one memorable encounter, a Russian soldier and a German soldier from World War II made an appearance at a mediumship-development workshop attended by their descendants. After receiving information about their deaths, it became clear that they had fought in the same battle. One soldier had died in an explosion and the other had survived. The fact that two former enemies were able to show up in peace was astonishing. Their presence was encouraging to many in the class, because it made the love, peace, and healing of spirit communication real.

In spirit, love for comrades in arms not only crosses international boundaries but also transcends different wars, and branches of service as well. (I know that this is particularly hard to believe if you've ever attended an Army-Navy game!)

This unifying camaraderie is illustrated by an encounter between a Navy vet in spirit who'd served in the Vietnam War and a young Army vet in spirit who had served in Iraq. Their meeting took place at a spirit circle in my office. After everyone had gathered for the event and found a seat, I noticed a young man in spirit standing next to a woman in the group. He gave me the feeling that he was her son. I heard the name James, and the mother acknowledged that her son James had died. It was easy for me to assume that he had died while in the Army; after all, he was standing there in uniform and I'd heard a gunshot. His mother also confirmed that he had died from a gunshot wound.

But then I heard the word *suicide*; and his mother said, "Yes, he died from a self-inflicted gunshot wound after returning from Iraq." Well, that wasn't what I expected.

Next, my eye was drawn to an older man in spirit, dressed in Navy whites. He placed his hand on the shoulder of a serious-looking woman sitting next to James's mother.

"It's not your fault that I died," the Navy man said after identifying himself as a therapy client of the woman, a therapist. This was an unlikely turn of events, as it is usually family members and friends in spirit who come to visit my spirit circles; clients don't tend to make the guest list. In this case, though, it began to make complete sense. This spirit, who had survived the Vietnam War, had taken his life only a couple of weeks previously. He had been under the therapeutic care of the serious-looking woman—her specialty was working with veterans suffering from PTSD.

The two veterans in spirit, both suicides, stood at attention next to one another and those who loved and cared for them. The Vietnam vet made it clear to his therapist that he would help and support her work with veterans. And the Army vet? Well, he wanted to be sure his mother knew that he was with his comrades in arms and not alone, and that there were people on Earth who could help her recover from his death. After the circle was over, I noticed the mother and the therapist in deep conversation; and I'm sure that this was only the first of many.

Servicemen and -women on Earth and in spirit share the concepts of honor and service. This was demonstrated by a spirit circle I was invited to do in Colorado Springs. As I drove closer to the house, a young man in spirit named Brad appeared in my car to show me the way. When I pulled up in front of the house, I mentioned Brad to the woman who met me outside on the sidewalk. She gasped, clutched her chest, and cried, "Brad is my son."

Among the many relatives and friends in spirit who visited the circle, Brad was very much in the center of things. Before the circle closed, Brad shouted and spelled "Thom! T-h-o-m!" without any further explanation. No one at the circle knew a Thom; and when I turned to Brad for more information, the only sense I received was that soon his family would understand the reference.

What I didn't know at the time was that Brad's family was attending a memorial for him and his fallen comrades that afternoon at a local military base. When his family arrived on base, forty to fifty cadets were present. Noticing the grief and confusion of Brad's family, a cadet separated himself from the group, walked up, and introduced himself as Thom. He offered to accompany the family to the ceremony. Brad's mom was shocked and made the strange request that Thom check the list of cadets to see how many Thoms were present. As ordered, he reviewed the list and reported back that there was only one other, spelled "T-o-m." "*You're* the right Thom, then," Brad's mom said. "My son sent you to take care of us." Thom didn't question the logic and took good care of Brad's family during the ceremony and afterward.

To sum up, when our servicemen and -women speak to me, whether they fought and died during a war or after, they speak of peace and connection to those who have also served and to those they love.

5

Afterlife Relationships

30. Do spirits know how much we love and miss them?

The answer to this question is an unequivocal yes! However, those we love in spirit don't mourn in the same way that we do. Why is this? It's not because they don't care for us; it's because they remain connected to us. For spirits, death doesn't create separation. However, we live in a physical world, which may make this concept difficult to understand or accept, so let me explain.

Many of us believe that death severs the connection with the people that we love. For spirits, however, living after death is living in complete and total connection to everyone and everything. Consequently, they don't see themselves as separate from us or from any form of life. In fact, in some ways, the connection is more intense and more real than it can be for us on the Earth plane. These different perspectives were illustrated in a succinct way when a young man in spirit said to his mother in a sitting, "I'm okay, Mom," and she responded with, "I'm not." That pretty much summed it up. Indeed, one of the primary reasons spirits make the effort to communicate with us is because they are okay, but they know we are not.

As a medium, my purpose isn't only to provide messages; it's also to teach others to develop their sensitivities to spirits. The ultimate goal of my work is to ensure that everyone (spirits and those on Earth) gets and stays connected. It might seem ambitious and possibly even strange that part of my work's mission is to make myself (and other mediums) obsolete. However, I am convinced that spirits are on board with this goal. A recent session illustrates this point.

"Please tell my husband that I love him," a young widow told me during a session.

"You don't need a medium to send your love to your husband," I replied. "When you think or say 'I love you,' your husband hears you directly."

Her husband in spirit showed me a bench by a mountain lake with a fishing pole leaning against it. "Oh yes, he used to go fishing on that lake," she confirmed.

"He's showing me a picture of you sitting on that bench, a fishing pole at your side, and Valentine hearts floating in the air around you, with 'I love you' written all over them."

Tears formed in her eyes.

"On Valentine's Day, I sat on the bench at his favorite lake with his fishing pole next to me. In my mind, I kept telling him, 'I love you.'"

At that point, she didn't have a doubt that her husband had received her love—and neither did I.

Death seems like such a big (and sometimes final) separation due to the loss of a person in physical form. On earth we're used to expressing our love by touching a hand, kissing a cheek, or giving a hug. The spirits live in a world of energy—that is their language. When we think about a spirit in a loving way, they receive the message. Love is one of the most powerful (if not the most powerful) energy forces in the Universe. Of course, it can cross any boundary—even death!

In some cases, not only do spirits feel the love we send to them but also our love helps them. One of the more dramatic examples of this was demonstrated during a phone session with Marsha and her mother in spirit.

"Your mother has a critical voice," I mentioned to Marsha.

"That's an understatement!" she retorted.

Her mother then asked permission to be part of the reading.

"That's the most respect she's ever showed me!" exclaimed Marsha.

At that point, Marsha's critical mother went on to catalog a number of instances in which she had trampled her daughter's self-confidence, apologizing in the process. She also confessed that she had always been jealous of the special relationship her daughter had with her husband. She went on to explain that her own father had shunned her as a little girl and it felt as though she was being ignored again—this time by her husband. That fear destroyed the potential for a loving relationship between her daughter and her.

"Mom never told me any of that—I didn't know," said Marsha in response.

"Thank you," her mother continued, "for showing me how to love. Thank you for forgiving me for the ways in which I hurt you."

Marsha confirmed that, with the help of years of therapy and spiritual work, she had forgiven her mother and worked hard in her own relationships to always express love and support. She was shocked to learn that in the process she had taught her own mother how to love. Then, in a bit of a twist, Marsha's mother mentioned her love of books and provided specifics about a book Marsha was under contract to write. After a surprised acknowledgment, Marsha's mother offered to help finish the book, which was about (drumroll, please) mother–daughter relationships! After a shocked silence, Marsha was able to consider the possibility of continuing the relationship with her mother in a new and different way.

Even if love wasn't expressed in a lifetime on Earth, it is never too late to learn to love and to share that love.

For more on the healing work of mediumship, read Q&A number 5, "What is mediumship for?" in chapter 1, "The Basics," and number 17, "If I don't get to say goodbye before I die, is it too late to do so after?" in chapter 3, "The Dying Experience."

31. Do spirits still feel love for us?

When we talk about love, it is often in reference to either a romantic or a familial relationship. In other words, the way we love our family is different from the way we express love to a boyfriend, girlfriend, or partner/spouse.

In the afterlife, however, distinctions between these types of love no longer apply. The fact that there isn't romantic love in the afterlife might be disappointing to some—it is hard to imagine what could be better than being in love! Well, love in the afterlife is an expansive love; instead of being in love with one person, we're in love with all that is, and we're loved by all in return. The BIG love that spirits live in is unconditional and limitless, and therefore rare in comparison to the love that we typically know here on Earth. It is a powerful and universal binding force.

It might be easier to understand Earth love versus spirit love if we think about it this way: On the Earth plane, love is a lifeline that connects us, ensuring survival. If we didn't love babies, what would happen to the next generation? Love also serves as an antidote to loneliness and separation. These conditions of survival are specifically related to the fact that we live in bodies that need to be sustained, especially when we can't take care of ourselves.

In the afterlife, however, the physical world no longer dictates the needs that earthly love must fulfill. The BIG love of spirits is expansive and encompassing, and less individually directed and conditional. All types of love shared on Earth are a fractured version of the magnificent, holistic love that binds the entire Universe together.

When I'm communicating with spirits, the love that they share with me is the expanded version, even when a husband in spirit is giving a message of love to his wife. Within the space of this expanded love, and beyond the limits of romantic love, there is room to bring healing to the pain caused by an affair or a divorce or death.

In the afterlife, the imbalances of love that we see here on Earth are brought into perfect balance. In the afterlife, those who couldn't give love finally can, and those who couldn't receive it finally do—a point that was made by a young man in spirit named David.

"He never felt at home in this world," I relayed to David's mom at a gallery-style reading event. David, who had given me the word *suicide*, had died only a month prior to the event.

"He is a lovely, sensitive soul who is so sorry for the pain he caused by choosing to die," I continued. David spoke about feeling like an alien while on Earth and not understanding why people were so cruel to one another.

As his mother continued to acknowledge the information being shared, I was startled to see David transform into an iconic superhero. "He looks like Spider-Man!" I exclaimed.

"That was his favorite Halloween costume," responded his mother.

As Spider-Man, David sprang from wall to wall above the people in the audience, webs shooting out from the tips of his fingers. This was a first for me as a medium and utterly surprising! *What are you doing? What are you showing me?* I asked him in my mind.

David responded with, "I'm creating a web of love over everyone here." He then gave me a vision of a web being cast over the entire Earth—the very place that hadn't felt like home to him.

As I explained what David was doing, the looks on many faces revealed that the love was palpable—not imaginary at all. David had demonstrated that the alienation he experienced on Earth was transformed by a bigger love, which he was dispersing from his side of life. And this young man's message gave me pause.

Several days later, as I continued to contemplate the experience with David, there were news reports of a mass shooting—another in a series of attacks on students. This was a reminder of the cruelty, violence, and hatred on earth that David found so difficult to bear when he lived here.

David isn't the only spirit from whom I've received messages of universal peace and love; some have offered it as an antidote to the sudden violence exploding into everyday life. Obviously, spirits report that they support their loved ones in times of personal difficulty and trouble all the time; but what I hadn't considered was that individual spirits could cover the *world* with that same love at any time. And if David is surrounding the world with love, aren't other spirits doing the same? What if that BIG love—the universal binding force—is available to us for the causes of good here on Earth? I think it is!

With a web (or grid) connecting spirits and people of goodwill, each one of us is empowered to imbue every situation on Earth, no matter how negative, with the love of spirits. Just like David, wherever we see cruelty on Earth, we can be the superheroes of BIG love. And we don't even have to squeeze into a skintight costume!

32. Does romantic love exist in the afterlife?

It makes perfect sense to ask (and hope) that the afterlife experience includes romance. After all, romantic love is one of the most inspirational subjects on Earth, often portrayed through poetry, song, dance, and art as the pinnacle, the height, the very description of bliss and expression. Well, I hate to be the one to dis your bliss, but romantic love, as we understand it, doesn't exist in the afterlife.

Before being *too* disappointed, consider for a moment that there are just as many songs, if not more, written about love gone *wrong*. While Taylor Swift fans dissect her songs, looking for clues about her latest romantic disaster, perhaps we should be grateful that romance in the afterlife isn't of the Swift "nightmare dressed like a daydream" kind.

That being said, I have no doubt that those who have asked about romance in the afterlife have been blessed by a beautiful, loving relationship that has been shortened by death. In these situations, it is heartbreaking to consider an eternity without romance when the desire is to be reunited with a loving husband, a devoted wife, or a longtime partner who has passed.

Often, when I'm asked about romance in the afterlife (which is *very* often), it could also be that people are too shy to ask, "Is there sex in the afterlife?" Let me cut to the chase on this front as well: there isn't sex in the afterlife either.

"What?! No sex? But I *love* sex!" exclaimed a friend in response to my informing her of the realities of the afterlife. After further discussion, it became clear that it wasn't just sex that she enjoyed but the sense of connection it brings, which sparked a long conversation about sex (I will spare you the details). After much thought, sharing, and laughter, we came to the conclusion that sex at its best is intimacy, comfort, connection, acceptance, joy, and fun; and sex at its ultimate is an expression of deep, abiding love. Of course, sex has to be good so that the species doesn't die out! (That's just my Capricorn practical side speaking.) By the end of our discussion, however, we agreed that sex is rarely just sex; it fulfills many needs.

The truth is that many of these needs die along with the physical body. First of all, there is no need to procreate in the physical sense. In addition, here on Earth, the physical body and all we dress it with is not only a personal expression but also a clear invitation or barrier between ourselves and intimacy with others. In the afterlife, all barriers fall away; and consequently, there is no need to practice a sexual act to establish intimacy. In the world of spirit, the higher vibration of love is an energy that flows like an electric current through *everyone*.

Leaving a dense physical body behind allows our energetic bodies (and the essence of who we are) to easily connect in love with other beings. In the afterlife, living without physical barriers allows for an energetic intimacy—a universal merging, connection, and joy. And don't worry; this doesn't mean that spirits live as one big blob! In unconditional love, there is oneness but also memory of an individual life and that life's personal connections. Within the oneness, there is still distinction and difference but without division and separation.

Let me reassure you that although romance and sex don't exist in the afterlife, earthly relationships are remembered and remain important. In speaking with spirits, they provide evidence that the intimacies of relationships on Earth are far from ignored. For example, as I was meditating prior to a phone reading, I sensed a husband in spirit who arrived with lots of questions—not questions *he* wanted to ask but those his wife wanted to ask him: "Is it okay to sell the car?" (Her husband loved his Mustang.) "What about the truck?" (Her father-in-law wanted it.) "How do I go on living without you?"

Some questions were a bit mundane and others heart wrenching, but her husband gave me answers all the same, sometimes providing the questions before his wife could even ask them. His concern for her was specific and detailed; and this, more than anything, demonstrated his love for (and continued interest in) her and the family.

And now back to sex. Spirits do bring it up now and again; however, when they do, it is often in the context of how their actions on Earth (while they were alive) continue to affect those they've left behind. One father in spirit insisted on speaking with his son about his (the father's) philandering, which had caused the dissolution of the family.

The son had been thinking about getting married but was afraid that, like his father, he would not be able to sustain a monogamous relationship. By addressing the disappointments and fears of each, a father in spirit and a son on Earth worked together to transform a legacy of hurt into one of love and fidelity.

In addition, spirits frequently demonstrate that they remember how much romance means to us on Earth. For example, a husband in spirit told me that he would show up with "hearts" for his wife. She confirmed that he was a diehard romantic and would surprise her at work with heart-shaped balloons, even when it wasn't Valentine's Day. During the session, her loving husband insisted that she could see hearts from her window at work. She looked at me like I was crazy. But at a subsequent session about a year later, this same lady told me that while looking out her office window, she noticed that the latticework on the building across the street had hearts in its design. Her husband is still surprising her at work with hearts!

Love *is*—it is never lost. It is there in the very structure of everything, even in the latticework of a neighboring building. Sometimes, especially when our hearts are broken, it is just hard to notice it. So spirits point the way.

33. Do spirits get jealous?

On the Earth plane, jealousy is often incorrectly equated to love. In other words, the love we feel for someone is equal to the intensity of jealousy that arises when an interloper threatens the relationship. But based on what I know from speaking with spirits who have been killed by jealous spouses or significant others (or even acquaintances), jealousy relates more to the idea of ownership than it does to love.

The idea of ownership—most especially the idea of owning another human being—dies with death. Marriage vows often state, "Till death do us part"; and when we say, "You're mine," here on Earth, that contract doesn't remain enforced in the afterlife. Spirits know this even if we don't; and because they know it, they can be quite inventive when helping to introduce new love into the life of someone they've left behind.

This was true in the case of a husband named Walter, who was also a big dog lover. As he lay dying, he asked his wife, Lisa, to take his beloved beagle for regular walks as he used to do prior to his illness. Lisa agreed. During our session together, Walter reminded Lisa of her promise; and she confessed that she missed her husband so much that she could barely get moving herself, much less get out and walk the dog.

"He needs to go for walks!" Walter stated emphatically, which seemed even a bit callous. After Lisa agreed to do herself and the dog some good, the session ended.

Years later, Lisa returned for another session at which Walter made an instant appearance.

"Your husband is showing me a dog with hearts around his neck for a collar. I keep hearing 'love' in my ear and the name Adam." Lisa started to chuckle.

"I wondered if Walter was going to bring this up. You probably don't remember [and I didn't] that years ago, my husband suggested that I take his dog out for regular walks. Well, I started taking him out twice a day. During our walks, I met other people in the neighborhood. One of those I met was a man named Adam who had lost his wife almost to the day that my husband had died. Our friendship has grown, and we now own a shared dog named Love." (I had no doubt that their shared love extended beyond a dog with that name!)

After the session, I thought about how wise and wily Walter was. He knew that his wife, in her pain following his death, wouldn't be open to the idea of meeting someone new. But he also knew she would be willing to keep a promise to him, so he let a dog lead her to a new love.

Another example of this unconditional love from a spirit occurred during a phone session, when I felt the commanding presence of a spirit named Johnny. When his wife, Janice, called, her husband affirmed his identity by providing specific details of their life together. But then, suddenly, in the middle of the conversation, he took a detour. He showed me a vision of his wife standing on a dance floor, inviting a thin guy with a ponytail and a plaid shirt to dance.

Janice went silent. After a few beats, she stated that I had described an actual event. A friend of hers, too shy to dance, had to be dragged out onto the dance floor. And with that, her usually garrulous husband in spirit got silent. "This isn't just a friend," her husband confided to me and then gave me the feeling of a budding romance.

"Wait a minute," I said to Janice. "You'd like something more with this guy . . . more than just a dance, right?"

"Yes," she said barely above a whisper.

For most people, this kind of conversation would fall into the category of awkward! For me, though, it is far from unusual. I speak to a lot of widows and widowers—of all ages—and spirits are almost always willing to bring up the subject of another love, because it is a difficult thing for a dedicated spouse on Earth to contemplate: *Is it okay to love someone else? How long should I wait before looking?* Spirits haven't given me a manual for finding love after the literal death of a marriage, and that's probably because there isn't a one-size-fits-all solution. This was the very dilemma that Janice was facing.

"Your husband gives me a feeling that you have reservations about this new relationship."

"Yes, that's true," agreed Janice. "In fact, that's why I'm calling you. Up until this point, I've felt Johnny around every day. As soon as I met

William [her new man], I didn't feel Johnny anymore. I figure that's because he's angry and jealous, because I found someone else! Right?"

I paused for a moment, not in reaction to her vehemence but so that I could hear what her husband wanted to convey in response. But even I was surprised by what he shared with me.

"Your husband wants to thank you for taking care of him toward the end of his life. He gives me the feeling that he could barely get out of the chair without your help. He needed your help to dress and bathe."

"Yes, that's true," Janice said.

Then I smelled alcohol and saw a snapshot of William in my mind.

"William has a history of alcoholism, correct?" I asked Janice. "He's just getting back on his feet and hasn't been sober long, correct?" I added.

"Yes, that's right," she confirmed.

At that moment, Johnny provided me with a flash of insight: "Johnny gives me the feeling that you feel at your best when you're taking care of someone else and that this new man needs lots of help."

"Yes, that's right. He needs help in every way, even financially. But I don't tell anyone that," she confided.

"Johnny tells me that you don't want to have to take care of anyone anymore—that this is your time for yourself."

"Yes, that's what I've been saying to family," she declared.

"Is it possible for you to allow the new man in your life to be responsible for himself?"

It was at this moment that she got the "aha!" that Johnny had led her to. His stepping back from the charismatic presence in her life each day wasn't about jealousy; it was about giving her the space to explore a new relationship and solidify the choice of leaving behind an ingrained role as caretaker. *Aha!!*

As Johnny and Walter know, love isn't finite; love is expansive and inclusive. We can love more than one person and, yes, be in love with more than one person—even have more than one soul mate—in a single lifetime. This doesn't mean, however, that someone is being replaced; what author Nicci French wrote in *Day of the Dead* is really true: "No one is ever like anyone else. No one can be replaced. Every death is the end of a world."[6]

What spirits want us to know is that each relationship is singular and sacred, but endless love also creates innumerable worlds. Both of these things are true, because jealousy is *not* the way of spirits.

> *For more on soul mates, read Q&A number 56, "Are soul mates a real thing?" in chapter 9, "The Big Questions."*

34. Can spirits intervene on our behalf?

In a variety of car-accident near misses, sitters have reported that they had the feeling to go down a different road or to turn at the last second. I experienced a near miss myself while driving through a national park on vacation. I heard a voice say distinctly in my ear, "Go slow." This was not an intuitive feeling but the voice of my mother in spirit. I took my foot off the gas just in time to avoid being hit by a kayak sliding off the roof of an SUV in front of me. (My mother and I were once in a terrible car accident together, so it isn't surprising that she would be the one to warn me.) If we are willing to be open and aware, spirits can direct our attention to danger. Being open and aware is simply living without (or with reduced) distraction. In my life, I've learned to be fully present in each moment of my life rather than obsessing about the past or feeling anxious for the future. (For the most part, I'm successful!) I also live in quiet surroundings—no TV, music playing in the background, or constant text interruptions.

It's important to note that even when we choose to live in open awareness, it doesn't mean that spirits can and will intervene to prevent every accident. If this were the case, we'd all live on Earth forever! However, it is often in times of great stress or trauma that we can become aware of the intervention of Good Samaritans or loved ones in spirit.

For instance, when a young woman shared the memory of her death with me, I saw a mysterious dark-haired lady in the vision. As the young woman lay dying by the side of a road, following a devastating accident, the dark-haired lady knelt beside her and held her hand. It would have been easy to assume that this was her mother, but her mother was in the room with me and didn't look at all like the lady in the vision. Despite the flashing lights in the background, blinking an obvious alarm, I felt tremendous peace.

"That is so weird," her mother said to me after I shared the vision. "I was told later by the police that a lady with dark hair, who said she was a nurse, stayed with my daughter while paramedics tried saving her life. After my daughter died, the woman couldn't be found to give a statement."

If this mysterious lady was indeed a *spirit* Samaritan, the intervention's purpose was to ease a young woman's passing into the afterlife rather than to keep her on Earth.

"I'm so relieved," said her mother at the close of our session together. "I couldn't bear the thought that my baby died alone." In effect, this intervention also eased the mind of a fearful and grieving mother.

Some spirit interventions can soften a blow, *literally*. During a session, a father in spirit informed his daughter that he had been present when her mother took a fall down the stairs. "It could have been much worse!" he exclaimed while demonstrating to me that he had gently supported his wife as she fell.

"My mother told me that she fell 'lightly,'" said the daughter. "Now I understand what she meant by that."

Interestingly, the fall was warning enough for her mother to install a motorized stair lift. In this case, a helping spirit hand released resistance and created the opportunity for an independent widow to accept mechanical help.

There are universal rules that govern the ways that spirits can interact and intervene in any situation. Perhaps the preeminent rule is that actions on the part of spirits cannot supersede our free will. That being said, there are times when people think that they're acting freely but, instead, are reacting to patterns inherited as family legacies. Fortunately, spirits know the difference between living in awakened consciousness and blindly following a pattern, even if we don't.

One of the ways that spirits provide support, most often for those in their family line, is to intervene on behalf of those dealing with inherited illnesses, like alcohol and drug addiction, diabetes, and depression. Spirits are particularly interested and able to help if they suffered in similar ways while on Earth. This is best illustrated by an encounter I had with a family for whom addiction was an intergenerational struggle.

As soon as I sat down for a small spirit circle with ten family members, I was overcome with the smell of alcohol from the spirits. One by one, the spirits introduced themselves; each had succumbed to alcoholism, with most dying from complications of the disease. As I was speaking with the spirits, one stood apart from the rest. He was standing next to what looked like a mountain still (an old-fashioned apparatus for distilling alcohol), and I heard the name "Wade Boy."

When I shared the information, one of the sitters gasped. She had discovered just that day that her great-great-grandfather, Wade Boylan, had made moonshine. So why were all these alcoholics in spirit with us at that circle? They were there to let everyone in the group know that they were helping the youngest male member of the family. His name was also Wade, and he was struggling with drug addiction.

"It is time to end this thing," Wade's grandfather in spirit said. "We're going to help this boy!"

Months later, I heard good news from the family: Wade had received a surprise grant from his grandfather's church to attend a rehabilitation facility that specialized in new treatments for addictions. As far as I know, he is drug free and doing well. I have no doubt that the relatives in spirit—from Wade Boy, who made moonshine, to the grandfather who died of liver disease—were the ones who inspired church members to help this young man.

Spirits are great counselors when it comes to choosing a profession as well. At a small spirit circle, a mother in spirit mentioned to her daughter that she should consider the jewelry business. "Jewelry?!" her daughter asked incredulously. "I don't have any plans to go in that direction." A year later, this young lady emailed me to say that "out of the blue" she had been offered an opportunity to partner in a successful jewelry business—and loves it!

Another mother in spirit gave me the sense that her daughter, Marion, felt betrayed by her employer. Marion confirmed that she had just been laid off after twenty years of work, and she was questioning whether or not all those years had been valued. As she looked for a new job, she was volunteering at an animal shelter; and Marion's mom encouraged her to continue volunteering there. I heard back from Marion months later that through the animal shelter, she met someone who hired her as a publicist for raising awareness about the plight of homeless animals. Now Marion loves what she does and works for a cause that inspires her.

Spirits can and do intervene, in small and big ways, but we have to do our part as well; spirits can't do for us what we can do for ourselves. They can, however, point us in the direction of healing, freedom, and purpose.

> For more on how spirit can come to our aid, read Q&A number 62, "Can spirits help us find peace after loss?" in chapter 9, "The Big Questions."

35. What is the best way to honor the memory of a loved one in spirit?

Historically, cultures have honored the dead with complex rituals. I experienced this firsthand when I attended the premiere of *King Tut: Treasures of the Golden Pharaoh* at the California Science Center in Los Angeles. It was the largest touring exhibition of tomb artifacts ever.

What I wasn't prepared for was how the objects from the tomb would impact me physically. As a medium, I've learned to ground and protect myself; however, my usual preparation wasn't enough to keep me from getting light-headed and dizzy, and needing to sit down. Each object, more stunningly beautiful than the last, was created and imprinted with great intent, and served a purpose in the king's journey through the afterlife. For example, the king's wishing cup, made of translucent alabaster, was carved with a wish that he be granted eternal life: "May your ka (spirit) live millions of years; may your eyes see wonderful things."

According to the ancients, a person died a second death when the last person on Earth who had spoken their name died as well. Building monuments to stand for the eons was insurance that one would not be forgotten. As I walked through the exhibit, I couldn't help but compare the pharaoh's expectations with what I've heard from loved ones in spirit.

While traveling in Maryland, I was invited to do a spirit circle at a lovely home. When I walked into the basement family room, illuminated and perfumed by a pumpkin Yankee candle, I noticed a mother in spirit standing next to who I assumed was her daughter, Linda. The spirit, though elderly, was full of energy. After she provided evidence, which included her name Ramona, the way she died, and a hobby of growing orchids, she suddenly disappeared and then reappeared across the room, standing next to another woman, Gina. (When spirits move during group events, I may see a fast-moving blur; I may also lose sight of a spirit and feel drawn [pulled] to turn my head to a place in the room where I'll see the spirit once again. This all happens quickly, so there isn't much lag in the conversation, as was true in this case.)

I addressed Gina by saying, "Well, Ramona now wants to speak with you, so I trust that you know her and the woman sitting across the room."

"Yes, I do," Gina responded.

"This spirit gives me the feeling of 'mother,' so she's your mother too, right?"

"Yes," she responded, a bit sheepishly. Everyone in the group laughed. Although I wasn't in on the joke, I found out later that the sisters wanted to sit separately as a "test" for the medium.

"I know that this might sound odd, but your mother wants to plan her funeral."

"Oh no, that's not strange," said Linda.

"Your father wants to have a big, fancy send-off to honor their life together. You agree with that," I said, pointing to Linda.

"You disagree," I said, pointing to Gina, "because Mom says that you know that she wouldn't want a big to-do."

"Yes, that's right," Gina acceded.

"Mom knows that your dad needs the funeral done his way, so don't worry about the money," I announced after consulting with their mother. Both daughters laughed. They then explained to a puzzled group and medium that their mother had died that morning. Their day had been filled with arguments about whether to support their father's plans or to honor their mother's wishes to save money by having her cremated and foregoing a funeral. Their mother solved the dilemma by supporting her loving husband's decision. Although spirits are not attached to funerals and memorials, or to whether they are cremated or buried, they recognize that we, on Earth, often need a concrete way to express our grief and love.

Oh, and one more thing: the reason the two sisters were at a circle on the day of their mother's death was that they had purchased the tickets for the mediumship event months before; and as the money-conscious sister Gina said, "We couldn't get a refund on the day of the event." Mom definitely used that decision to her advantage!

These days, funerals have given way to celebration-of-life ceremonies; buying real estate for burial sites seems less important. People are pursuing all kinds of creative options for honoring loved ones. I smile when I remember a message given by a loving husband in spirit to his wife: "Feed the fishes in Hawaii," he asked me to tell her. His wife explained that her husband used to joke that when he died, he wanted to be fish food. In fact, she had already planned a trip to Hawaii two weeks after our session to release her husband's ashes at sea. Needless to say, she was delighted that he knew about it.

As previously mentioned, spirits seem to be unattached to the details of funerals and memorial services, as their focus is on how they support those left behind. At a gallery-style event, a young man who had died at the hand of a shooter on a killing spree showed me a huge crowd at the celebration of his life. His mother confirmed that more than two thousand people attended. Her son expressed that he was glad that so many people in attendance helped his mother to know that his life had made a difference to each of them.

Spirits even like being remembered as a team sport! "I'm seeing a baseball game," I mentioned at a spirit circle to a petite brunette named Alma. "The players on both teams have a photo of a young man on their shirts. Stunned, Alma paused and replied, "Next week is the second annual memorial game for my son, who died on the field. The two teams had shirts made with his photo on the front."

A young woman in spirit named Lexi suggested another popular way to be remembered. She said to her parents at a sitting, "I want to be remembered with growing things," and showed me a snapshot (in my mind) of a bench surrounded by a garden. Lexi's mother confirmed that her daughter had volunteered at a botanical garden and that a memorial bench with a plaque bearing her name was placed by the beds of roses.

Even pets get into the act! During a recent phone session, I mentioned to a woman that her dog, Skipper, wanted to be remembered as she ran along the beach. Interestingly enough, Skipper was a stray she met while running on the beach one morning—and they ran together every day until he died.

Some families choose to honor a loved one in spirit by creating a foundation not only as a remembrance but also to do good in the world. I'm reminded of a session during which a young boy in spirit showed me a bright, shiny red bicycle, red helmet, and matching red balloons. This picture was in response to his mother asking, "Adam, do you know what we were doing this morning?" Before coming to see me, Adam's mother and father had been distributing red helmets and balloons at an event for children. After their son, Adam, had died from a head injury sustained while riding a bike, they made it their mission to provide helmets (in their son's favorite color) to children in need.

And foundations aren't only for the young. When a loving wife and her two stepchildren came for a sitting, her husband and their father made it clear that he knew about the foundation in his name and commended his son for how he is handling the distribution of money for museum art installations.

Remembering loved ones in spirit, however we choose, helps set up and maintain a connection of love that transcends death. We don't need to remember spirits to keep them alive; we need to remember them to keep us connected to them. The act of remembrance infuses our continuing relationships with nothing less than the power of eternal love. So, when remembering someone you love, in whatever way you choose, be assured that they will be present with you in that moment and always.

36. What is the difference between guides and angels?

I would sum up the difference between guides and angels by saying simply this: guides speak on behalf of our human potential, and angels speak on behalf of all that is divine.

Defining the differences between guides and angels, however, is a bit of a daunting task. As a medium, I take each spirit—whether guide or angel—as an individual and not a representative of *all* members of their group. It is also important to note that others may have vastly different experiences with these spirits, and as a result, present different descriptions. There is tremendous diversity among spirits, and I appreciate and celebrate that fact.

As a medium, my primary purpose is to provide evidence from loved ones in spirit that can be validated in some way; communicating with guides or angels provides a different challenge altogether. Evidence of their existence is often anecdotal or based in personal belief; and it's influenced by legends, literature, and religion. What I know for sure about guides and angels is a result of personal experience. Remembering my encounters over the years brings a smile to my face. This is because meeting entities from each of these groups of spirits is not only fun (and sometimes funny) but also provides a greater glimpse into the workings of our Universe, most of which goes unnoticed and unseen in daily life.

Although guides and angels are spirits, one of the differences is that not all of them have experienced life in a physical body like ours. The angels I've met do not speak of lives on Earth; some guides, on the other hand, do. And guides for whom Earth was never home, and who may be from different dimensions and universes than ours, in my experience, are aligned with people devoted to channeling wisdom from the highest frequencies of existence.

However, the fact that most guides have lived on Earth can be a comforting fact. It is important that a spirit who is guiding us through this life *gets* what life entails. Who wants to take a trip with a guide who hasn't visited the tourist attraction? Not me!

My first memorable interaction with guides was early in my career. I had just done my first large public event, which had gone surprisingly well. (At least it was surprising to me!) As a result of the success of the first event, a second was immediately scheduled. When sitting with my friends, who were also mediums, one of them informed me that the spirits told him that I would be getting a new guide for the next event—a "trainee."

"A trainee," I shrieked. "I need a professional!" However, the purpose of a trainee guide soon became clear.

Following the event, a medium in the audience told me that she saw guides surrounding me as I was providing messages. While I was speaking with a young man whom the spirits indicated was going to be a working medium soon, one of the guides moved from beside me and stood next to the young man. In the months following, this man, who was in his late teens, became one of the youngest professional mediums in southern California. And then I got it! The trainee guide worked with me so that he could go on to support the work of another medium. From that time on, mediums have reported seeing the same thing happen at other events; guides leave my side, ostensibly to support the work of others.

This network of guides is vocational—one of the subsets of guides who help each of us with our work. Teacher, accountant, scientist, and mediumship guides help and inspire teachers, accountants, scientists, and mediums on Earth. Doctor guides help surgeons, direct researchers to cures, and help healers to use energy effectively. Creator guides work with artists, musicians, writers, and others who live in imagination and make fantastic worlds come alive, soothing our souls and inspiring us. Native Americans in spirit work with shamans and Spiritualists, and I have witnessed a Zulu warrior serve as gatekeeper and protector guide to a medium about to step into national prominence. Children and babies who have died in the womb (or soon thereafter) are often joy guides, even to those like me, who have never been pregnant! These precious joy guides bring laughter and fun to ordinary and stressful times alike. They are reminders that joy is never really gone; it's just misplaced or unnoticed. When something ridiculously funny happens, a mischievous joy guide is often behind it! I have met all these types of guides—not only my own but also the guides of those who study with me or have a session with me.

There is a far-reaching and interconnected network of guides who help us here on Earth. In fact, I can confidently say that *nothing* happens on Earth without there being a spirit component to it. The implications of this statement are astounding, I know, and possibly hard to accept. And yet, the longer I work as a medium, the more evidence I see that the Universe is peopled with spirit helpers.

Many assume that loved ones in spirit are present in their lives as guides, and they ask me if this is so. Well, as the interest in guides and spirit communication increased in popularity, I observed something interesting, not once or twice but many times. Here's an example.

A lovely young woman named Genevieve, dressed in bohemian high fashion with blond, highlighted hair cascading in salon-worthy waves down her back, sat down in my office in great distress. Her father in spirit, a successful businessman, provided me with specific information about his sudden death from a massive heart attack and the extensive business empire he had left behind. As this talkative spirit continued, I could feel a shift in the energy of the room. I glanced around and saw a golden, glowing figure moving toward the young woman on the sofa; I heard "guide" in my ear. Whenever a spirit identifies him or herself as a guide, I know that a sitter has asked for guidance. Guides have never shown up uninvited to a spirit family visit.

With confidence, I said to Genevieve, "You came today hoping for guidance," and then added, "guidance about an acting career," as I noticed a vision of a stage appearing in front of her feet.

"Yes," she said, a bit surprised. "I was hoping that my daddy could help me in my career." And then I saw the "something interesting" I mentioned earlier: the golden, glowing figure leaned in close to Genevieve's father and spoke to him directly. After that exchange, he began to communicate to me about his daughter's talent with great enthusiasm, providing encouragement. Genevieve left the session with a list of projects and steps to consider in the coming months.

After the session, I reviewed what had happened. It was an odd encounter, particularly because spirits don't have to whisper to one another to communicate; that action was almost "stagey" in its presentation. Perhaps this was because Genevieve desired to work as an actress? However, I also think that Genevieve's creative guide was demonstrating that a guide will enlist the help of a loved one in spirit if necessary. Who would trust guidance from someone unknown, golden, and glowing? It is far more likely that Genevieve (and anyone, for that matter) would take a serious message from someone recognized and loved. (Oh, and by the way, guides don't always appear to me as golden, glowing figures; sometimes, they come as monks, doctors, musicians, and even animals, including elephants, jaguars, and giraffes.)

This example illustrates another thing about guides: they don't require that we know who they are. When meeting one of my own guides during a meditation, I asked for a name, and the guide's response was, "No matter."

Angels, on the other hand, announce themselves: Michael, Gabriel, Uriel, Raphael, to mention several. When I first started seeing angels during events and sessions, it was in the context of a loved one in spirit who was religious or collected angel figurines. Eventually, however, I started seeing angels with sitters who didn't consider themselves religious but spiritual. In all cases, whether sitters considered themselves religious or not, the angels appeared as large beings, not always clearly male or female, and unexpectedly without wings. Inevitably, the sitters had preestablished relationships with one or more angels and were interested in communicating directly with them. In my experience, angels are willing partners who communicate in declarative sentences. I always know when an angel is speaking; it is like opening an email written in all caps. And the message is not yelling, exactly, but clear, precise, and powerful.

These days, not a week goes by without me seeing angels and guides along with loved ones in spirit at events and sessions. When these guides visit, they bring messages of living life at the intersection of love and greatest possibility. When angels visit, they speak of love, joy, peace, and protection—they are the messengers of the divine.

I am seeing angels with ever-increasing and somewhat stunning frequency. This may be because there are serious threats to life on our planet. However, these are also times of great connectivity, with momentous opportunities for change and transformation, both personal and global. The presence of the angels indicates that the highest frequencies of creation are here on Earth and therefore accessible to us. Their presence may be an urgent request that we listen—and learn.

> *For more on animals as guides, read Q&A number 48,*
> *"Do animals in spirit help us in our lives?" in chapter 7,*
> *"For the Love of Animals."*

37. How can I meet my spirit guide?

I have found that there are times when it can be encouraging and comforting to meet and get to know the spirits on your team. If you would like to develop a more interactive relationship with your spirit guides, as I have, a visualization meditation is a simple and effective way to be introduced.

Rather than trying to remember the following meditation, it would be helpful to record the text on your phone (or in some other way); then practice the meditation as the recording plays back. If you are doing this exercise with a group, a designated reader can lead the meditation.

Spirit-Guide Invitation

* Find a quiet place.
* Sit upright in a straight-backed chair, with your hands resting comfortably on your lap, palms facing up.
* With your eyes closed, pay attention to your natural breathing—in and out, in and out, in and out.
* Once relaxed and comfortable, allow thoughts to pass by without fixating on any one. Return your attention to your breathing if you get distracted.
* Take a moment to consider what questions you would like answered by a guide. Allow the questions of your heart to rise naturally:

    > Do you desire clarity of purpose?

    > Are you hoping to feel comforted and supported?

    > Is there a project for which you need direction?

    > Are you seeking guidance in beginning or continuing a spiritual path?

* Once you feel settled in your intention for the meeting, bring your attention back to your breath.
* Continuing to keep your eyes closed, begin the visualization . . .

Spirit-Guide Visualization

Imagine that you are standing on a beach of white sand. The sun is bright and warm and a gentle breeze tickles your skin. Looking across turquoise waters toward the horizon, you can see an island with a hill rising out of the sea.

As you walk along the beach, you come across a small boat and get in. The boat glides effortlessly and soundlessly toward the island. When the boat reaches the island's shore, you get out and start walking toward the hill.

At the base of the hill is a shiny red park bench, and you sit down. As you relax there, you can feel the bench's deep red color moving through your body, from your feet to the top of your head. After allowing yourself to experience the grounding energy of red, stand and begin walking toward a gently sloping pathway, which leads to the top of the hill.

At the start of the path, there is a large, glowing, translucent orange ball. Place your hands on the ball and allow the bright orange color to fill your body, from your toes to your head. As you do this, you may even smell the cleansing scent of citrus. Anything you don't want to carry with you on your journey can be placed in the glowing orange ball for safekeeping. Do you have any troubles or concerns weighing you down? If so, you can leave them here, feeling lighter and less anxious.

As you continue walking up the hill, you notice the yellow sun and feel its warmth filling you from your toes to your head. Pause for a moment and enjoy the sun on your face.

Continue your walk up the pathway, which begins to curve. As you come around the bend, you find yourself at the edge of a dense, lush forest. The leaves on the trees above and the ferns along the side of the path are various shades of green. Pause for a moment and breathe deeply. Allow the living green color to fill your body. Wherever there is discomfort, disease or heartache, the green will soothe and bring healing to it.

Do not be surprised if an animal or two joins you on your journey. Allow them to appear on their own terms. They may not be forest animals, but that's okay.

As you continue walking along the curving path, the trees part, and you find yourself high above the ocean, with a view of a cloudless blue sky. Let the blue of the sky fill your body with a sense of peace about communicating with your spirit guide or guides. As you continue enjoying the blue sky, drop your eyes to the horizon—to the indigo line of division between water and sky. Allow the indigo to fill your sight and your body. You may feel lighter, as though you have left all cares behind.

At the summit of the hill, there is a cave with two pillars of amethyst, their rich, violet color standing solidly on either side of a shadowed opening. And in front of the cave is a white alabaster bench. You find yourself drawn to the bench, where you sit down to rest. As you sit, allow any questions you may have to rise to your mind. Questions not previously considered may arise, but there is no need to speak them aloud. Simply express thanks from the heart for the opportunity of this meeting.

Without expectation, allow one or more guides to be revealed at the mouth of the cave. The encounter may last for a moment or for several. Silently give thanks again for the meeting.

You may receive information from your guide(s) as thoughts, symbols, or visions; you may hear answers to your questions in your mind; or you may hear this wisdom audibly. Allow yourself to be open to the ways in which your guide(s) communicate with you.

When you're ready, arise from the bench, take note of any animals that remain with you, and begin your descent down the hill. Look out toward the horizon, and notice it thinning between the water and sky.

As you continue walking down the path, enjoy the expanse of the cloudless blue sky. Walking through the forest, allow the cool green of the shading leaves to fill you. Your companion animals may choose to remain in the forest.

Leaving the forest behind, you feel the sun warming your back as you return to the orange ball at the foot of the hill. Take a moment to consider whether your troubles are best left behind in the safety and security of this ball.

At the bottom of the hill, take a seat on the red bench, allowing yourself to feel warm and at peace.

You look to the shore and notice that the boat is there, waiting for you. You walk to it and get in. Effortlessly, the boat leaves the island behind and gently returns you to the pristine beach of white sand.

You step out of the boat and begin walking along the beach, returning to the place where you started.

Pay attention to your breathing once again. Feel yourself in your chair, with your feet on the ground and your hands on your lap. When you're ready, open your eyes.

* * *

Practice this visualization meditation as often as needed. It may be helpful to write about your experiences in a journal so that you don't forget the details. You can also use it to compare different visits with your guides, revealing where you've been and serving as a chart or map as you continue exploring your spiritual path.

The animals you met in the forest may also be guides. The work of Dr. Steven Farmer—in particular, his book *Spirit Animals as Guides, Teachers, and Healers*—can be helpful as you work with these guides.

If you didn't see a guide the first time, don't be concerned; *be patient*. As you become more comfortable with this meditation, it becomes easier to make the connection. There may also be times that you sense a presence rather than actually see a guide; or perhaps you hear an answer to your question(s) without seeing who is giving you the information. As with any relationship (human or spirit), the key is to allow it to develop naturally, with time.

6

The Language
of Spirits

38. Is there a "veil" that separates the living from the dead?

As long as I've been communicating with spirits (which is almost my entire life), I've heard from other people about a "veil" that separates beings on Earth from those who are celestial; it is a wall of sorts between this life and the afterlife. I've never actually seen this veil, although others report having seen it and felt it. Among paranormal enthusiasts and practitioners of ancient traditions (paganism, Wicca, and so on), it is commonly accepted that the veil is thinner during Halloween festivities, allowing for all sorts of spirits (sometimes undesirable and frightening) to break through. This historical belief is supported by increased reports of ghostly sightings and paranormal activity during the month of October—reports that continue to this day from my clients and other spirit communicators, as well as the general public.

However, after years of experience with ghosts and spirits, I began to question the entire idea of a veil between the worlds of the living and the dead. Once in spirit, they're present; they don't step out dramatically from behind a curtain, as though a show is about to begin. While having tea with a friend who is also a medium, I asked her opinion about the veil. "Maybe it doesn't exist," she suggested. And I think she's right!

And yet, if that is true, why is there a persistent sense of a division between life on Earth and life in the afterlife? Quite simply, I think it is because we believe (and maybe even need to believe) that there is one. But before you start imagining demons running amok in the world, let me explain.

When I provide messages from loved ones in spirit, I set the energy for communication at the frequency of love. At this frequency, only spirits who have our best interests at heart are allowed to participate in the work. A father in spirit appeared during a gallery reading event and stood at a door of the banquet room. He would not (or could not) enter the room without permission from his son, who was attending the event (and whom he had abused). The spirit made it clear to me that he had changed; however, his son wasn't ready to hear from his father. As a result, the spirit did not enter the room.

This is only one example of a boundary set by love that allows for those living on earth and in spirit to meet in a space of mutual respect. Yet it also demonstrates what I've long suspected to be true: that the veil is actually a wall of fear and anger that we have built to keep away anyone we think will continue to hurt us.

Over the years, spirits have driven me to the brink of abandoning the idea of any separation. In the past, my mediumship development workshops were called "Touching Two Worlds"; however, now that it has become so clear to me that spirits do not recognize that their world and ours are separate, I have named my workshops to reflect this understanding. Workshop titles such as "Life with Spirit," "Spirits of the Heart," and "Cocreate a Life with Spirit" demonstrate how my work supports the idea of a collaborative and unified connection between people and spirits.

This is not to say that we, who are incarnate, have an all-access pass to every vibrational plane of spiritual existence. The limitations of our physical existence constrain the expansion of our consciousness. There are simply frequencies at which we can't vibrate—our physical bodies can't take it. In this sense, spirits have an advantage: they can be in more than one place at a time, and can adapt to a far greater

range of vibrations and frequencies. Fortunately, they're willing to retain their connections to us despite our limitations.

So what happens if we let go of the idea of a veil between two worlds? Well, then we will be compelled to let go of our fear of death and all that entails. But the release of this fear invites the possibility of cocreating a life on Earth with spirits as an integral part of that life. Spirits aren't mere observers; they'll participate in our lives if we allow it.

When people prepare to come to an event or a private session, I suggest that they invite loved ones in spirit to attend. In actuality, an invitation isn't necessary; spirits are already here. The invitation process, therefore, is really for *us*. In thinking about those with whom we desire connection, we're acknowledging that we're ready to hear from them. The blocks of fear, loss, anger, grief, guilt, and blame all crumble beneath the great weight of willing love.

So, who is in control of the veil? *We are.* Spirits already know it doesn't exist, and they've been waiting for us to acknowledge it too. All we need to do is release our personal veils of fear and acknowledge that the love of spirits surrounds us, and they are here to guide us.

39. Is it true that spirits can visit us in dreams?

This is probably the most frequently asked question of all the questions in this book! It even beats out Q&A number 32, "Does romantic love exist in the afterlife?" In order for this to be the single most popular question, many people must be dreaming about loved ones in spirit.

It is indeed true that spirits can visit in dreams; and in fact, dream visitations may be the one consistent way that spirits make an appearance to people of all religions and cultures.

Historically, dreamtime and connection with the unseen world is acknowledged and respected. Native Americans value dreams for guidance and connection to the spirit world. Carl Jung, founder of analytical psychology, viewed the language of dreams as central to his work. Edgar Cayce (aka, the "sleeping prophet"), who is also widely respected as the father of holistic medicine, provided messages of healing while in a sleep-like state. The dream researcher and theologian Dr. Kelly Bulkeley sees dreams as a "primal wellspring of religious experience." His book *Big Dreams: The Science of Dreaming and the Origins of Religion* casts dreams as important to the evolution of religion and spirituality as a whole.

Spirits find dreams an easy and effective way to demonstrate their presence. This is simply because, while sleeping, we're in a receptive state in which we're not telling ourselves what isn't possible! Spirits take the path of least resistance. Research shows that brain waves (beta) of cognition (when we're thinking) and those of dreaming (theta) are different. Spirits can also make use of the presleep (alpha) and hypnagogic states, which occur while falling asleep and starting to wake. Auditory visitations—literal "hellos" from spirits—can be heard in the state between sleeping and waking, during the theta-alpha bridge. So with all this dreaming going on, it might be helpful to know what differentiates a dream visitation from an everyday (or should I say, *every night*) dream.

At events when I'm asked whether a dream might be a visitation, I usually respond with another question: "What did the colors look like in the dream?" One lady said in response, "The colors were so vivid and intense. I've never seen colors like that before." A saturated "supernatural" palette is one indication that a dream is a visitation. Conversely, spirit dream visits can also seem completely natural, without any special lighting effects. When a friend visited me in a dream, he and I were sitting at my kitchen table, drinking tea and chatting. It was so real that I woke up having to go to the bathroom, which is what usually happens after I drink tea! Spirit dream visitations are also different from dreaming, in that they're hard to forget. As I was writing this answer today, my friend Joan shared with me that her father visited her in a dream when she was twenty-four. More than twenty-five years later, she still remembers every detail!

The fact that so many people experience dream visitations can make some wonder, *Why don't I see my spirits in dreams too?* Let me assure you that it isn't because spirits don't want to visit; grief often disrupts the sleep cycle. At the very moment a connection is desired, stress can interfere with sleep patterns essential for spirit visits.

To help with sleep challenges (falling asleep and staying asleep), practice relaxation exercises before going to bed, such as lying down with your feet elevated, and alternately tightening and releasing all the muscle groups in the body. Don't watch the news or other nervous-system agitators during the evening, and turn off all technology at least an hour before bedtime.

Speaking of sleep patterns, don't worry that we're keeping spirits up at night. Remember, they don't have bodies that require sleep to rejuvenate. In other words, they're not up all night visiting with us and taking naps during the day to catch up. And inviting a loved one in spirit for a nighttime visit is simple: just thank him or her for trying. (I have no doubt that they are.)

One of my clients was delighted to discover that these suggestions actually work! After several days of relaxing before sleep and practicing gratitude, she had her first dream visit with her son. Up to that point, she had despaired that it would ever happen—and the visits continue to this day. Her son appears healthy and happy (despite dying of a debilitating illness); in one dream, they even shared ice-cream sundaes. Other times, she sees him standing with other family members in spirit.

Not all dream interpretations seem positive at first. For example, I received a distress call from a lady whose husband was convinced that when his parents showed up in his dreams, it meant that he was going to die. As his terror increased, so did the concern that he would become unhinged due to lack of sleep. Fortunately, during a reading, it became clear that his parents were visiting to support life changes he needed to make to improve his health. It was their son's life, not his death, that was their concern.

Another misinterpretation that causes unnecessary distress is if a spirit in a dream doesn't say anything. "Is my dad mad at me?" one worried sitter asked after having such a dream. My answer to her (and to you, if you've dreamed in a similar way) is *no!* Just showing up is a spirit's way of saying hello without saying a thing. Sometimes a spirit will appear to be crying in a dream, yet numerous times, spirits have shared that these are tears of happiness at being reunited.

Loved ones in spirit may not look exactly like themselves when they appear in dreams. A mother told me that she met a spirit that was bright white and glowing in a dream; and although the spirit didn't look like her son, she knew it was him. That feeling of certainty— that knowing—is also an indication that a dream is a visitation. When doing a SiriusXM radio show with John Edward, a caller's uncle in spirit identified himself by name, and gave the message that he had visited in a dream but appeared differently. When John asked the caller what that meant, she replied that he was dressed up in the dream rather than wearing his usual flannel shirt. I guess her uncle thought a spirit visitation was a formal occasion!

If the idea of dream visitations interests you, it may be helpful to keep a dream journal. This practice of writing down *all* dreams will not only foster spirit connections but will also make you more aware of your unconscious thoughts. Recognizing patterns in your dreams will help you to differentiate between a spirit visit and wishful dreaming.

These days, sleep is a hot health topic; so it shouldn't be surprising that with better sleep, my clients and workshop participants are reporting more spirit visitations. The best advice from the spirits and me? Go to bed, and get ready for a visit!

40. What are the signs that a spirit is present?

The presence of a spirit can be subtle; and it is easy for us to dismiss a breeze across the face, a whisper in the ear, or a slight indentation on the bed as figments of imagination. That being said, please know that loved ones in spirit never give up reaching out to us, nor do they lose patience when we miss a sign. Even so, it is important to hold up our end of the "conversation." Understanding how spirits make themselves known allows for ongoing communication.

At a private family spirit-circle event, a grandmother in spirit, the matriarch of the family, gave a message to each member of her family. Messages were so specific that it became clear that she knew exactly what was going on in the life of each person in the room.

"I see a little house over your head, which is the symbol for real estate, and I see books at your feet," I reported to one granddaughter. "It seems as though your grandmother knows that you might be going to school for real estate." The granddaughter gasped and confirmed that she was starting classes in a few days to become a realtor.

With each of her children and grandchildren, this grandmother, who "held the family together," commented on the new diet being tried by one, the upcoming wedding of another, the retirement of her son, and the distribution of her jewelry and estate to all. She was either the busiest spirit in the Universe, flying around from one family member to the next, or her connection with everyone in her family was unlimited and omnipresent.

Without the restrictions of a physical body, in a world of expanded consciousness, spirits can be around us and our entire extended family at the same time. It's a bit like the spirit version of Facebook Live: each person is in a separate location, but communication and connection are simultaneously possible—physical distance isn't a factor. I think that one of the reasons this grandmother demonstrated her omnipresence was to dispel any concern on the part of her relatives that any one of them might "hog" her attention.

Loved ones in spirit can also choose to concentrate their energy to appear to the eye or to physically affect things on the Earth plane. This concentration of energy happens not only during sessions with a medium but when spirits reach out directly to anyone on the Earth plane. For example, when I mentioned to a client that her young son in spirit was holding a red balloon, she told me that at her son's recent celebration-of-life party, a single red balloon chased her around like a game of tag. I have no doubt that her son had concentrated his energy to playfully move the balloon.

When we call on spirits in times of need, or when we want guidance, the message is received. There is no need to worry that a message has gone astray. During meditations and sessions, I have seen actual lines of energy connecting people to spirits and to one another; these energy connections appear like glow sticks. And there have been times when these tubes of light are so interconnected that it looks as though everyone (spirit and person) is connected to everyone else. When I'm communicating with spirits during events and sessions, these networks of family members and friends can bring together some surprising groups. One woman named Melissa was surprised when her mother in spirit, who had passed years ago, appeared at a session with her best friend, who had died just the week before. "They didn't know each other," Melissa said, quite puzzled.

"They do now!" I told her, and continued: "You are the connection between them in the network."

This "framily" (friends and family) network allows for connection and communication between generations of spirits, as well as spirits within and outside of a family; and its lines of communication are open 24/7. This is why I say with confidence that we can't miss a message from spirits, nor can they miss ours. These messages are repeatedly being sent back and forth.

This being said, there are times when we are challenged as recipients; and it seems as though there is no help, guidance, or support coming from the spirits we love. Even though that is the way it seems, I assure you that this isn't the way it is. If there is a breakdown in communication, it is on our end! Whenever we feel ignored and alone, it may be that we're expecting an answer to arrive in a certain way. This is why so much of my work as a medium is teaching others how to get and remain connected to spirits. After all, there is no way that all the mediums in the world can collectively be the receivers and conveyors of *every* message! What we *can* do, however, is help you learn how to plug into your own spirit networks.

It is my belief that we are *all* wired for spirit connection. Although mediums may have a specific talent for spirit communication, there are things everyone can do to increase opportunities for personal spirit interaction. As a teacher, I like to keep things simple; so if you want to become more receptive to the messages and guidance of spirits, here are some daily habits that can help anyone feel more connected every day. (This is a condensed version of the practice from a series of online classes I teach. For more information, check out my website: HollisterRand.com.)

* **Grounding:** This means being fully in the body, in the present moment, and connected to the earth. Naturally grounding activities include:

  > Wiggling your fingers and toes upon waking in the morning

  > Walking barefoot on the grass

  > Gardening

  > Eating root vegetables

  > Sitting at the root of a tree

* **Gratitude:** Reminding yourself of the good things in your life creates a welcoming and expansive energy, which is helpful for receiving messages from spirits. Easy ways to introduce gratitude into your daily life include:

  > Reading a book about gratitude

  > Saying "thank you" a lot

  > Keeping a gratitude journal

  > Lighting a candle of gratitude for a loved one in spirit

* **Silence:** Allowing for blocks of time with no distractions can make room in your life for hearing the gentle guidance of spirits. As difficult as it may be to unplug from our frantic daily lives, consider ways to introduce more silence and presence. Some ways include:

> Sitting quietly and resting for a few minutes a day

> Meditating and allowing thoughts to drift by without attachment

> Limiting distractions around you and in your home

> Refraining from constant texting or surfing on the internet

* **Imagination:** Spirits use the function of our imagination to communicate, and exercising natural creativity can help prepare you to receive spirit messages. Try engaging your natural creativity:

  > Trying finger painting, coloring, drawing, and so on

  > Shifting perspective and going outside of your daily routines and habits (i.e., taking another route home than the usual one)

  > Taking a fun and creative class (e.g., pottery, painting, sculpture, and so on)

  > Noticing details that you might usually ignore and allowing yourself to be drawn in to their beauty (e.g., architectural, botanical, celestial, and so on)

  > Playing a musical instrument or singing (you can listen to music too)

* **Paying Attention:** By being receptive and attentive, and keeping a record of anything and everything you think might be a hello from spirits, you can build confidence in your ability to receive messages. Keeping a list of signs, thoughts, or messages can help you discern patterns of connection. Communications from spirits may come via:

> Electrical anomalies

> Seemingly random songs playing at a meaningful moment

> Number patterns appearing repeatedly on clocks or other places

> High levels of synchronicity that are surprising yet significant

Once you're properly tuned in to the network, you'll learn that spirits love technology and anything electrical. Lights flickering, TVs turning on and off (or changing channels to a favorite show), photos appearing on a computer screen, and random texts are all signs that a spirit may be present. I know this because my clients have extraordinary experiences like these for which their loved ones in spirit claim responsibility. Great-grandmothers in spirit, who shouldn't know an email from a tweet, talk about laptops and online business. Spirits are adept at communicating electrically, indicating a possible correlation between spirit communication and the fact that our bodies on Earth are electrical. Synapses "spark," the heart contracts at the prompting of an electrical pulse, cells in the body send electrical communications between each other—*all* seem a natural precursor to electrical communication between spirits and humans. It is a language without words.

Experiencing the presence of spirits is usually surprising—spirits catch our attention when we least expect it! This is demonstrated by what a woman shared with me after I reported her son in spirit showing me a closet door: "My son was always full of surprises. He used to love to hide in closets and jump out at the perfect moment. Maybe I shouldn't have been surprised when the pantry door flew open for no apparent reason on his birthday."

When we think we feel the presence of a spirit, it is important to trust that feeling. Feelings may seem vague indicators of what is real or not, especially in a culture where thinking is often given greater value; however, in assessing the presence of spirits in our lives, feeling or sensing is an effective gauge.

This feeling sense is known as *clairsentience* (French for "clear feeling"), and it is defined by Merriam-Webster as "perception of what is not normally perceptible." This sense is located in the center of our chests and commonly referred to as the heart chakra. When we lose someone we love, the heart chakra can close down or become dormant, which is a natural, self-protecting act when wounded by loss or trauma.

Fortunately, in the presence of spirits, the heart chakra may begin to open again and in a gentle way. When I'm communicating with spirits, my heart can expand with so much love that it is difficult to breathe. One of the ways I know that spirits are present is that swelling sensation in my chest.

Finally, it is important to remember that communication with spirits is interactive. Not only can physical objects be moved (have your keys gone missing and mysteriously reappeared?) but our bodies may respond as well. Have you sensed the presence of a loved one in spirit and gotten goose bumps as confirmation? Has "someone" tugged on your hair or played with it? Have you been "tripped up" by a pet in spirit?

It may take some time before you trust the feeling that those you love in spirit are around you. However, by practicing the above daily habits of connecting, and acknowledging feelings and physical interactions, we can know, without doubt, that those we love in spirit are not only alive but also distinctly present.

41. Can spirits hear our thoughts?

Yes, loved ones hear our thoughts but only those thoughts that pertain to them or have "hashtags" for topics in which they're experienced and interested. Our loved ones do not read our minds every moment of every day; that would be invasive, and spirits are quite respectful. In fact, if there's one major complaint that spirits have, it is that we don't leave enough space between our thoughts in which to hear their replies!

It is estimated that the average person has between 50,000 and 70,000 thoughts per day—that's a lot of thinking. Obviously, most of the thoughts are recurring to-do lists: get groceries, load the dishwasher, take the dog for a walk, and so on. In comparison, thoughts like *What can I do to support my sister as she struggles with cancer? How can I help my son heal from his addiction? Is going to nursing school the best option for a new career choice?* are invitations for guides and loved ones in spirit to inspire, support, and guide us. And receiving that guidance can be as simple as creating just enough space between our own thoughts to allow spirits to get in some thoughts of their own. A daily meditation practice is one of the best ways to create space for hearing from spirits. Just a few dedicated minutes in which you sit quietly, allowing your own thoughts to pass by, can be enough to begin a dialog with loved ones in spirit.

Spirits love to let us know that they're listening. There are frequent LOL moments during sessions, when spirits add to a conversation for which they've been silent listeners. For instance, a group of girlfriends came to a circle and one's mother in spirit said, "Get the red shoes." There was a group gasp and then laughter. The spirit's daughter explained to me that in the car on the way to the circle, she and her friends were discussing whether she should buy a new pair of shoes in black (practical) or red (flashy). Her mother was a fashionista and a shoe collector, so of course she voted for red!

We don't need to shout in order for spirits to hear us. During one private session, a husband in spirit promised his wife that he would support his son's recovery in rehab. "I'm so glad to know that," she told me. Her husband in spirit, who had died of alcoholism, was determined to help his son change his life for the better.

His wife confided, "I've been walking around the house saying out loud, 'Honey, our boy needs your help!' and my neighbors probably think I'm crazy!" I let her know that although we don't need to speak out loud for spirits to hear us, some people prefer to, because it helps them to state things clearly and concisely.

In a recent session with a widower, he said with tears in his eyes, "Would you tell my wife that I love her and always will?" I reassured this devoted husband that his wife in spirit could hear his thoughts of love already—*no one* ever needs a medium to send love to spirits. And be assured that they send back their love as well. Love is always a direct, two-way conversation.

Another thing to keep in mind is that spirits may also change their way of communicating over time. Many of my clients report extraordinary spirit signs following the death of a loved one, but obvious communications dissipate over time. If this has been your experience, let me first assure you that this phenomenon isn't related to a lack of interest or caring on the spirits' parts; it is simply because loved ones in spirit acclimate to the norms of their energetic life.

Think of it like this: if you were to relocate to another country— England for instance—after a while, your American friends might find it difficult to understand you, with your adopted British accent or slang. Spirits find themselves in a similar situation: we expect them to communicate like us and yet, with no physical voice boxes, hands, and feet, they can't! And the longer they're in spirit, the more they speak with energy, like other spirits.

This is where mediums and learning about spirit communication can help. These days, sessions frequently include a conversation about the signs and hellos that loved ones in spirit are sending. Sitters express concern that loved ones have "moved on," "crossed over," or in some other way, "left the building" (so to speak). Fortunately, my energy as a medium allows spirits to reacclimate their energies to those of the Earth plane, and following a session the communication between people and spirits is often increased. This isn't magic; it's simply giving the spirits a human communication refresher course.

We also have to do our part to become aware of how communication changes over time. During waking hours, spirits will use the energy available and circumstances in our lives to let us know that they're with us. However, it is important to note that if we are expecting a loved one in spirit to communicate in one specific way, we could be limiting the opportunities for connection.

For example, during a session with a woman named Melanie, she expressed great distress over not feeling her sister in spirit around her when asking for her help in getting a job.

"Soon after my sister passed, crazy things would happen with my laptop," Melanie told me. "Since my sister was in IT, I just knew it was her. These days, though, she doesn't seem to be around as much."

As I paused to get a sense of how Melanie's sister would respond, a picture of an iPhone flashed into my head. "Your sister is showing me an iPhone," I said. "I'm seeing a game on it—could be Candy Crush or something."

Melanie laughed and replied, "I was playing Candy Crush the other day, while waiting for a job interview, and kept scoring. I was killin' it!"

Melanie stopped suddenly and her eyes widened.

"Just as I had a massive explosion on screen, a girl walked by, talking on her phone, and said my sister's name."

In this ingenious way, Melanie's sister was letting her know that she was with her for the interview. And now that Melanie is no longer expecting her sister to only say hello with her laptop, she will be more aware of her sister's presence.

Because I'm a medium, people think that I've got an edge on connection when it comes to my own loved ones. Well, maybe that's true, but not in the way you might think. Often, hellos come in much the same way as they do for everyone, just a bit more on the extreme side.

For instance, I asked for guidance and support for writing my next book—this one, in fact. Later in the day, while running errands, I stopped at the library to return some books and pick up others. As I got out of the car, a swarm (yes, a *swarm*) of dragonflies flew around me with lightning speed. I'd never seen so many at one time in one place! After a WTF moment, I realized that my request was being answered in a *big* way—and at the library, of course. Not only were spirits there for me in the book arena, they also demonstrated a bit of humor with a dragonfly version of *The Birds*.

Loved ones in spirit are connected to us every hour of every day. By allowing their communication to evolve, we can enjoy the presence of spirits in a more joyful, consistent way.

42. Do spirits come to us as insects and animals?

"A hummingbird came right up to my face and then—*pfft!*—took off. 'Mom,' I said to the hummingbird, 'you've got to talk more slowly; I didn't understand anything you said!'"

This story was relayed to me during a session after I mentioned that a mother in spirit would use hummingbirds to announce her presence. I was quick to explain to the sitter that her mother hadn't *actually* become a hummingbird! But her eyes opened wide, and she still seemed shocked.

"Don't spirits come as birds?" she asked.

They don't, and I went on to explain.

Loved ones in spirit announce their presence by *influencing* birds and other kinds of animals and insects, not by becoming them. Family pets are particularly susceptible to the presence of spirits, for example. While getting my hair cut one day, my stylist mentioned that her dog barks incessantly at a dried wreath of roses from her grandmother's funeral. She is absolutely convinced that her dog sees her grandmother there.

During a session in a high-rise resort in Lake Tahoe, I mentioned to a woman that her husband in spirit said he would announce his presence with hawks. "Absolutely," she agreed. "Not a week goes by without a beautiful hawk appearing in the sky." No sooner had she said that than a hawk floated up past the window on an updraft. We were both stunned into silence.

I'll never forget the time I mentioned to a widow that her husband would use ants to say hello. "Oh, he's done that already, *big* time," she said. "Yesterday morning, I walked into the kitchen and screamed when I saw a line of ants on the counter. When I looked more closely, I noticed that they were walking around a canister, creating the letter "U," which is the first letter of my husband's name." (And I can honestly say that this is the *only* time I've heard that ants can spell!)

Whales, dolphins, and other sea creatures will respond to spirit energy as well. "Your son tells me he swam with you and the turtles," I said to a mother during a spirit circle.

"Oh yes!" she exclaimed. "My son always loved turtles. When we had a memorial swim for him in Hawaii, the turtles swam with us. They wouldn't leave." She then pulled a turtle pendant from under her sweater, which is her daily reminder of that spectacular experience.

Even flowers, plants, and trees respond to the energy of spirits. "Your son is telling me that you will hear his voice in the trees," I mentioned to a grieving mother. "I already have," she replied. "When I went camping with the family, I heard my son talking and laughing with the wind in the trees." And during a gallery-style event, a favorite aunt in spirit got a laugh from her niece when she took credit for a houseplant finally blooming after years of being dormant.

The stars in heaven can announce the presence of spirits too. At a barbecue, I was out on the deck with a friend whose wife had passed at age forty. "She was like a shooting star," I said, and at that moment, a shooting star lit up the sky. My friend saw it too.

Do I think that his wife became that shooting star? No, I do not. Do I think that she inspired us to speak about her just before we saw the star shoot across the sky? Yes, I do.

Loved ones in spirit aren't the turtles, the hawks, the hummingbirds, or the shooting stars. They are, however, willing to use any possible avenue of influence to let us know that they are with us and continue to love us as they always have.

For more on animals in spirit, read chapter 7,
"For the Love of Animals."

43. Do flowers have a special significance to spirits?

Funerals have flowers—*lots* of them. So it is easy to assume that flowers might have significance to spirits. But let's not forget that flowers are a meaningful part of many celebrations—birthdays, proms, weddings, births, and of course, Valentine's Day. In my work as a medium, I've noticed that flower references are plentiful and tend to relate to a particularly personal family story—even if a death is part of the story.

For example, during a session in San Diego, the aroma of roses suddenly filled the room. "I smell roses," I mentioned to Martina and her daughter, who were sitting with me and their mother/grandmother in spirit. As the conversation continued, the aroma of roses persisted. When I mentioned it again, there was a pause while Martina took a deep breath. Then she turned to her daughter and explained: "You don't know the story. When your grandmother died, the smell of roses filled the room. At that moment, we knew that she was letting us know that she was okay and still with us."

Spirits continue the traditions of marking many occasions with flowers and flower references. "Your aunt is showing me a large Christmas cactus with gorgeous red flowers," I mentioned to a woman at an event in July. "I knew it was her!" she exclaimed. This response came after a somewhat lengthy message from her aunt in spirit, who had an exceptional green thumb. The woman went on to explain that her aunt had given her a Christmas cactus that hadn't bloomed for years. However, immediately following her aunt's death, the cactus burst into spectacular bloom.

"I see pictures of flowers in front of me—daisy, lily, geranium, and violet," I mentioned to a woman who had just taken a seat in my office.

"I can't believe it!" she exclaimed while laughing so hard that she began to gasp. When she caught her breath she explained, "My grandmother loved flowers and gave all of her daughters flower names.

I thought, *Really? Geranium, not Rose?* and got a quick answer back from the grandmother in spirit. "Rose was just too common," she informed me. "And Gerry liked her name." Well, not only did her granddaughter confirm this, the spirit also put me in my place!

Spirits may sidestep the work of a medium and use flowers to announce their presence directly to loved ones. At one small family spirit circle, each person in attendance received a message from spirits that had a flower reference. A grandmother in spirit showed me an enclosed porch full of African violets. A mother in spirit flashed into my mind her prized and pampered orchids. But the most dramatic was a field of sunflowers that a sister in spirit projected onto the screen of my mind's eye. In response, her sister who attended the circle, related the following story:

> As children, my sister and I used to enjoy standing among the sunflowers that grew in the side yard. We loved roasting the seeds. The sunflowers were ours, and our mom and dad let us be in charge of them. Shortly after my sister died, I was driving to her house to pack up her things. I was crying so hard that I couldn't see the road. I pulled off the highway and felt compelled to turn down a country road. As I crested a hill, there were sunflowers as far as I could see. The shock stopped my

crying immediately! Of course, I had to get out of the car and stand among the sunflowers. A feeling of peace came over me. There is no doubt in my mind that my sister was right there with me.

The innumerable flower messages I've received over the years makes it impossible to ignore the importance of flowers in spirit communication. With that in mind, I would like to suggest ways in which you can use flowers to connect with your loved ones in spirit directly:

* Keep favorite flowers in a vase near the photo of a loved one; you might find that activity in the area increases. I've had reports of photos tipping over repeatedly and the flowers lasting far longer than expected, or even changing color.

* Pay attention to flower essences. For instance, if your grandmother loved lavender, make note of the times you smell lavender. The aroma may waft by on a significant calendar date.

* If you're given flowers as a gift, pause a moment and thank loved ones in spirit for remembering you! Flowers that a person is inspired to give may, in fact, be a favorite of a loved one in spirit.

* Spirits—particularly, the young in spirit—mention wanting to be remembered with "growing things." Therefore, planting memorial trees and gardens is appreciated by spirits, and are also great for the Earth!

44. Is it easier to feel the presence of spirits when near water?

A young woman told me at an event that when she was at the beach, she could feel the presence of her best friend, who had died in a rip current. At one point, she thought she saw her friend running along the water's edge; and she was concerned that maybe she was hallucinating!

Reports like this come my way with astonishing frequency. Some people might assume that this is because I live in southern California and the ocean is a major part of our culture. I know for a fact that this isn't the only reason. My clients are from all over the United States and Canada, and throughout the world. Spirit connections near oceans, rivers, lakes, waterfalls, or ponds are plentiful and consistent around the world.

Spirits like to share fond memories of times spent near water. For example, when a woman sat down for a session, I told her that I saw the image of a young boy and an older man with fishing poles in a rowboat out on a lake. "The boy is waving," I said, smiling.

"My father used to take Kyle, my son, fishing," the woman responded, returning my smile. "Kyle always used to wave as I watched from shore." As she finished the sentence, her voice suddenly broke, and a tear slid down her cheek.

I looked over her shoulder and saw her father placing his arm around Kyle. "You asked your father in spirit to take care of Kyle, didn't you?"

"Yes," she whispered.

Once again, I saw a vision of the boat, the lake, and the two fishermen. "They're fishing together as they always did," I told her. "Your son still waves to you when you're on shore."

As she was leaving, Kyle's mother told me that she visits the family home by the lake as often as possible. "Sometimes I think I see Kyle and my father out on the water," she confessed. It's important to note here that not only is Kyle's mother *really* seeing what she thinks she is seeing but also that it is happening in the present time. Her loved ones in spirit are creating new memories with her, not simply playing out something that happened in the past.

The energy near water is conducive to connecting with spirits. Many clients have recounted experiences in which they've met those they love in spirit on the beach while vacationing; and several have told me about spirit and ghost experiences on a cruise ship.

This is one of the reasons why I prefer doing events and teaching workshops in cities near a coast or in the vicinity of lakes and rivers. The negative ions generated by running water, pounding surf, white water in a river, or waterfalls enhance our moods by increasing serotonin in the brain. With even a subtle lift in mood, which causes a shift in grief, we can become more aware of a spirit's presence.

Being near water ramps up natural psychic abilities as well. Innumerable people have reported increased sensitivity at workshops in Hawaii, the Bahamas, Virginia Beach, and along the California coast. Even the act of taking a shower can cleanse personal energy fields and allow inspiration. Some of my best ideas and insights come to me in the shower. Have you ever had an aha moment in the shower as well?

Our bodies are up to 60 percent water (with the largest concentrations in the lungs at 83 percent, and in the brain and heart at 73 percent) allowing us to resonate naturally with the ebb and flow of tides and tidal waters.[7] This is the primary reason why during mediumship-development workshops, I use the movement of water in meditations to build the energy for spirit communication. Spirits frequently appear in these meditations, supporting the idea that they, too, relate not only to water in its actual form but also to its power as a symbol or metaphor.

When you feel the urge to spend a day at the beach, retreat to a mountain lake, or trek to the falls, spirits will join you! In fact, you may feel their presence without any effort at all. However, for those of you who would like a little help to tune in to loved ones in spirit, here is a meditation for connecting while near water:

* Step into the water, and allow your feet and toes to sink into the sand. Or sit comfortably upright onshore.

* Close your eyes and listen to the sounds of the water. Taking your time, pay attention to the auditory nuances of the water; each wave caresses the shore differently, and water plays over river rocks in variations.

* Thoughts of your day or a to-do list may invade your tranquility. Allow the sounds of the water to wash away all your worries.

* Keeping your eyes closed, you may have an internal vision of a loved one in spirit or receive an answer to a life-guidance question in thought.

* When you open your eyes, allow them to stay slightly unfocused. At the horizon or at the water's edge, you may see an image or fleeting glimpse of a familiar person in spirit.

Spirits honor our willingness to take time out from the busyness of our lives and will show up in moments of quiet—especially when we allow the power of water to connect our world to theirs.

45. Is it possible to communicate with our ancestors?

These days, sessions and events are pretty much Ancestry.com conventions. This is a relatively new phenomenon directly related to accessible and affordable DNA testing, as well as the easy exchange of this genealogical information worldwide (via the good ol' internet).

Even grade school students are exploring their genealogies, as I learned recently during a phone session with a father, Ryan, and his son, Jordie, a fourth grader. Ryan was delighted to be spending time with his mother in spirit—*and* her extended family. Nonnie and Papi were there, as was his favorite uncle, who had recently passed. In the middle of all the hubbub, the name Betty was also shouted out by a spirit, so I mentioned it.

"Aunt Betty is my father's aunt," Ryan replied. "We don't know much about that side of the family."

Well, Aunt Betty wasn't willing to sit back.

"Aunt Betty is showing me a family tree, with the branches on her side all filled out. You're doing a family tree, right?" I asked Ryan. (I knew that he must be, because when a spirit trots out the image of a family tree, they're in on the process.)

"Funny you should ask," Ryan replied. "I'm helping my son put together a family tree for a school project. To make it easier, we were only including people on Mom's side," he confessed. "Aunt Betty won't be on it," Ryan added.

At emphatic prompting from Aunt Betty, I declared, "Oh, she wants to be included. After all, she's part of this family!"

Aunt Betty's grandnephew and I had a laugh, but she made a point worthy of remembering: just because we may not know all of our ancestors doesn't mean that they aren't involved with our lives. And when we reach out to one ancestor or to one side of the family, in effect, our invitation extends to *all*. In other words, we can't uninvite members of the family to the party of life any more than we can excise their DNA from our own.

Interest about the ancestors in our lives is well expressed by the Seventh Generation philosophy, which is credited to the Iroquois Confederacy but actually practiced by many Native nations. The philosophy states that tribal elders consider the effects of their actions and decisions for descendants seven generations into the future. The understanding is that everything we, as humans, do has consequences for something and someone else, because we are all ultimately connected to all of creation. That means that the future lives of great-great-great-great-great-great-grandchildren are being taken into account by their ancestors. (And I can't even plan what I'm having for lunch tomorrow!)

In some cultures, it's not just acceptable but *imperative* to remember and honor ancestors. I'm reminded that during my time in Asia, I came to appreciate that ancestors are revered and consulted as a part of everyday life. It shouldn't be surprising then that with ancestral spirits thinking about us long before we were born, and our interest and veneration for them, there would be a synergy of connection.

Early on in my work as a medium, I was puzzled when a relative who may not have been known or liked would arrive during a session. It soon became clear that spirits weren't present just because the sitter ordered them up; there was an intent and an agenda that was independent of the sitter's apparent needs. However, in every single instance, that spirit was bringing a message of deep and profound healing.

You see, centuries ago, you were thought about; every time a child is born, legacy is born too. Ancestral spirits recognize their part in creating your physicality (eye and hair color, for instance) and setting into motion what is now present in your life (for example a proclivity for alcoholism). (I shared some of my thoughts about this with Dr. Steven Farmer, who interviewed me for his book *Healing Ancestral Karma: Free Yourself from Unhealthy Family Patterns*.) It makes sense that in learning about our ancestors, we are seeking to understand ourselves—we want to know where we've come from; we want to know where we belong and to whom; we want to know why dairy makes us flatulent. Ultimately, we want to understand our part and know how we fit in the grand scheme of things, starting with family.

This point was made a bit dramatically at a spirit circle not too long ago. Toward the end of the circle, I turned and met the eyes of a young man sitting directly to my right. As I scanned the space behind him, a panoply of spirits came into view and surrounded him. Because of this, I knew that: (1) he had a sensitivity to spirits himself, and (2) he had one whopper of a huge family!

"You're sensitive to the spirits," I stated. "When I see lots of spirits with a person, that is an indication that he or she has mediumship talent," I explained. "By the way they surround you, I get the sense that you've been seeking their help—asking for direction in your life. The reason I say this is that spirits have divided themselves into groups, and each group shows me a road. There are three roads ahead of you—three career choices, it looks like. Oddly enough, these roads merge, so I'm being shown that your work may be a hybrid, probably in the healing realm, because there are herbalists, spiritual healers, and religious prayer warriors standing with the group of ancestors." (I'd barely taken a breath as I reported the possibilities that the spirits were showing me.)

"Yes, there are three career paths I'm considering." He reeled off three medical specialties.

"Your spirits are giving me a sense of something a bit less traditional that could be a good fit for a healer like you—a body, mind, spirit approach."

"Oh, yeah, I've taken a look at integrative medicine, but my grandmother wants me to go to medical school and become a neurologist." With that statement, the spirits took a step back, and a number of them fairly bristled.

"Well, I am the last person to suggest that medical school or higher education isn't a great goal. In fact, I come from a family of educators. However, I see that the spirits have more to say here. Shall we give them a chance?" He agreed.

The first group of spirits was made up of Native Americans from at least two tribes. "I'm seeing Indians behind you," I reported. (Oddly enough, ancestors often refer to themselves as "Indians" rather than the politically correct term, *Native Americans*.)

"Yes, my mother swears that we are part Native American," he acknowledged.

"Absolutely!" the friend attending the circle with him exclaimed. "I took a photo of his sister, and she totally looks Native American," she added.

With that, I noticed another group of spirits moving forward. "Now I'm seeing a group of darker-skinned people (they didn't identify a race); and I'm smelling rum and hearing the names Johnson and Jameson. Lots of 'son'-type names here."

"Yes, I know what that is," he acknowledged. "My grandmother on my mother's side of the family is African American."

"They are very devout people," I continued, "sincerely religious but not Catholic. Looks more simple than Catholic."

"They were Methodists," he clarified.

"The Irish are over here," I said, as I heard the names Mary and Margaret above a background of Irish fiddles; and he confirmed, "My father, who I didn't know, was Irish and Ecuadoran." (Whew! Like I said—a *whopper* of a family.)

As the three groups of ancestors and I stared back at one another, in my mind, I asked to understand what they needed me to share.

Why were they all present?? And then, *bam*! They hit me with it: as the ancestors turned all of their attention to the sitter, I felt their pride.

"On your mother's side of the family, you're the first to go to college."

"That's right," he acknowledged.

"I can feel the pride of your entire family," I continued, barely able to explain the swelling of the pride in my chest. And yet, as I said this, I could also feel a sense of burden—a weighing down of my spirit. "But this may also feel like a burden, as though you are the one who has to do this for the entire family—those living and everyone who came before you."

"Yes, that's right," he said. "I feel like I can't do what I really want to do because it would disappoint everyone."

In this moment, it was a bit stunning to see the ancestors step forward in a unified front. I could feel a pressing down on my body and my spirit. "Your ancestors are giving me the feeling that you have come from a background where all have been oppressed—the Indians, the African Americans, and the Irish-Ecuadorans."

He looked at me with surprise—the latter was apparently something he hadn't considered.

"Yes, even the Irish were oppressed—by the English and then here in America, where there were signs saying, 'No Irish need apply,'" I added, knowing this from my own family history. "The ancestors are here to let you know that their oppression need not be yours; but instead, your freedom to choose is for them to share."

His sigh of relief was echoed by the ancestors in spirit.

When I say that you could have heard a pin drop at that point, I mean it—and my conference room has carpeting!

After the circle was over, I had a chance to speak briefly with this young man. He shared his excitement about a future in which he could use his talents and abilities without the burden of carrying the entire ancestral line on his shoulders. Now he knows that he stands on the shoulders of healers and those connected to God, to hard work, to education. The ancestors both freed him and lifted him up.

So yes, it is possible to ask ancestors for insight. And actually, from their side of things, they may well be asking, "What's taken you so long to ask for our help? We're here!"

Remember, your ancestors stand ready and waiting too.

> *For more on how mediums bridge different languages, different religious beliefs, and even different time periods, read Q&A number 8, "Can mediums communicate with spirits who speak a different language?" in chapter 2, "On Being a Medium," and Q&A number 57, "If my loved ones reincarnate before I die, will we miss seeing one another in the afterlife?" in chapter 9, "The Big Questions."*

7

For the Love
of Animals

46. Can the spirits of pets communicate through a medium?

Thankfully, they can and they do. My life is much richer for having met innumerable animals in spirit, including a dancing iguana that lived in a frat house, a miniature donkey that loved poetry, and a German shepherd that died a war hero. I'm amazed by the personalities, quirks, devotion, and brilliance of animals. However, I recognize that not everyone reveres them as I do.

People (usually those who don't have pets) seem surprised that animals in spirit are able to communicate with me. An attendee at a large event challenged me by saying, "Maybe I'll accept that you can talk to people in spirit, but animals? How can you possibly understand them?" (Humans are also animals, but I didn't feel the need to state that fact.) Anyway, much to his surprise, I explained that animals not only use words to get their points across but also pictures that they project into my mind.

Fortunately, I'm not the only one who accepts that animals can think and also communicate with words and symbols. There's the gorilla named Koko, who learned American Sign Language and famously shared her feelings about the death of her pet kitten; a border collie named Chaser, who was taught the names of more than one thousand toys by his person, a former professor named John Pilley; and then Alex, the famous African gray parrot, who seemed to understand exactly what he was saying, according to the animal psychologist Irene Pepperberg. Scientists are discovering that animals have a far richer emotional life and grasp of language than was previously thought. Of course, if you're an animal person, you already know this!

In my experience as a medium, Alex the parrot, as impressive as he was, had nothing on a spelling-champion terrier in spirit named Snickers. When Snickers started spelling out words like "o-u-t" and "t-r-e-a-t" during a session, her owner and I had a good laugh. Snickers had allowed her person to think that she had been outwitted by spelling out favorite activities. Not so.

Thinking about dogs and food makes me smile. "Food! Food! Food!" was all that Bella, a black Labrador in spirit, wanted to talk about during a gallery-style event. She showed me a movie in my head in which she would make the rounds in her Colorado Springs neighborhood, scarfing down any treats offered by proprietors. But when it came to table scraps? Well, that was another story!

"Bella says you're a vegan," I mentioned to her person.

"Yes, I am," she replied, proud that her dog appreciated her refusal to eat animal products.

"Bella is letting me know [and there was a dramatic pause here] she wasn't a fan of leftovers." The audience was in hysterics, as was I. Bella was a carnivore and not afraid to own it.

The importance of pets was highlighted in a 2015 Harris Poll, which indicated that more than 60 percent of US households have a pet, and 95 percent of those consider their pets family members.[8] In some cases, a pet may be a person's *only* family. For example, during a spirit circle, I hesitantly reported to a young woman, "I don't see any people with you today, but there is a beautiful white rabbit in your lap."

I wasn't sure how the sitter would take this information, but my deal with spirits is that I give what I get—nothing more, nothing less. In this case, I wasn't ready for what happened: The young woman began to sob so intensely that she could barely catch her breath. The specific and detailed messages the rabbit shared made it clear that their relationship was one of the only bright spots in the woman's troubled life. At that moment, I learned that *it is not possible to overestimate the value of a relationship with an animal of any kind.*

Pets (just like people) in spirit remain interested and involved in our lives; and the exuberance with which animals communicate from the afterlife astounds and delights me. Then again, sometimes it is the first time that they have had the opportunity to say what has been on their minds for years, as well as express their love in human terms.

In some instances, pets communicate in startlingly human ways. A spirit named Sadie told me how much she enjoyed riding in the truck with Jody. She showed me a picture in my mind of two people sitting upright in the cab of a truck. It wasn't until Sadie turned her head and I saw her snout that I realized I was talking with a dog—a labradoodle, in fact.

"She thought she was human," I told Jody.

"We always used to say that Sadie was a human trapped in a furry body," Jody replied.

I would say that Sadie agreed.

Animals in spirit can be honest—sometimes brutally so. I discovered this when a man put a leather collar in my hand at an event and asked me to connect with his beloved pet. Imagine my surprise when a monkey, not a dog, made an appearance.

"He says that he is a little man. I know that he's a monkey, but he does look like a tiny person as he stands next to you," I told his "father."

The collar, which looked as though it belonged to a large dog, did not seem fitting for the monkey. However, the man informed me that his monkey (who was called "Little Man," by the way) had worn the collar around his waist.

During a subsequent message, Little Man commented on the new monkey in the family by saying, "He's not as smart as I am." The man and his family agreed with that statement. Little Man was opinionated and had lots to say about their daughter's tattoo (WTF?), the new pool (not big enough), and a possible move to a ranch (great idea—lots of room for more monkeys). As I said, Little Man was brutally honest.

Mediums aren't the only ones who communicate with beloved pets in spirit. When I mentioned to a woman that her golden retriever in spirit was trying to play with her Pekingese, she laughed. "Penny (the Pekingese) will just stand there barking at air," she said. "Then she'll grab her toy and start running in circles." Penny could see what her owner could not.

Pets in spirit will play with us as well. Items like socks may go missing. (Ever wonder where all those socks go?) Pets in spirit also continue to join us in our daily routines. A springer spaniel in spirit told her person, Alma, that she enjoys walking with her every afternoon. Her one complaint, though, was that the new dog, a Pomeranian, would demand to be carried when she got tired. (Yup, brutally honest.)

Tucker, a Chihuahua-terrier mix, claimed to be able to jump onto the bed now that he was in spirit. (He had been banned from the bed after breaking his leg when jumping down.) His person then told me, "Last night, I noticed a Tucker-sized indentation on the quilt. Before going to sleep, I thought I felt him lick my face. I concluded that this was just my imagination playing tricks on me, because I miss him so much." Tucker made it clear that he was still up to his old tricks.

The deep bond we share with pets makes the decision to end their suffering a devastating one. When animals communicate in spirit, they almost always address this painful choice. For example, at an event, a German shepherd arrived with opera music in the background; her name was Lola. Lola went on to tell her person/mother that she loved the sausage treats but not the ones that were bought on sale with coupons. Her mother laughed at being busted. Lola went on to tell her mother that she could hear her crying at night because of the decision she made to release Lola from her body. Lola thanked her for making that choice, because she hated that she could no longer walk and was making messes in the house.

Unlike us, animals don't fear dying. They do, however, speak of a contract they have with us; it is no coincidence that the right pet comes into our lives at the perfect time. A loving animal will stay on Earth beyond what is physically bearable, until we are willing to release him or her to spirit. Many more times than I can count, animals in spirit have thanked their owners for allowing them to go on to a life where there is no pain and where they can run again (after being crippled here).

At this point, I'm speaking also of what I know personally. There was once a love of my life named Chi. He was an F4 Bengal, which means that he was only three generations away from wild Asian leopard cat origins. Chi was gorgeous to look at, with his leopard-like rosettes, and his eyes were wise, with a hint of rebel in their greenish hue. When my sister stayed with me one summer, she was somewhat terrorized by Chi's athleticism, prompting him to leap the length, not the breadth, of the bed she was sleeping in.

For nine years, Chi was the only man in my bed. (Okay, maybe a bit sad, but true.) So when Chi wouldn't eat one day and became increasingly listless over the next few, I was panicked. As I told the emergency vet, "This is just not like him."

After a weekend in emergency care, with a tube inserted in his stomach and a dismal prognosis, I brought Chi home. The veterinarian had outlined some options for keeping Chi alive—all of them invasive and none of them with even a midlevel percentage of survival. As I sat on my bed, holding Chi in my arms, I asked him, "What do you want me to do?"

A distinct and crisp voice in my head answered this question with, "If I were in the wild, would I still be alive?" Because I'm a medium, you might assume that nothing much surprises or startles me, but his answer certainly did. I have no doubt that, in that stressful moment,

Chi was letting me know that his wild DNA had a commonsense answer I didn't want to accept. At four that morning, I contacted a mobile vet and emailed my friends. Chi was surrounded by those who loved him as he died.

You know, of course, that this isn't the end of the story. Death *never* is the end of the story, after all.

The weekend following Chi's death, I had agreed to teach a mediumship workshop, though I wasn't sure how I could possibly get myself together for it. (For one thing, for the first time in nine years, I was sleeping alone, which meant that I wasn't sleeping.) On the second day of the workshop, one of the participants asked to share with me an unusual dream she had had the night before. She described a handsome man dancing flamenco in a leopard vest. He said in the dream, "I'm her man," and then he held up a picture of me! "What could this possibly mean?" the student asked me.

I was gobsmacked. In that moment, I ceased being the teacher and became a bereaved pet person. What this workshop participant didn't know is that I called Chi "my man" and we used to dance together every day. I would pick him up, he would put his front legs around my neck, and we would dance. If I were giving out stars for achievement in spirit communication that day, this participant would have gotten a hundred. This also brings up the point that our pets hear what we say about them and honor that relationship, as ridiculous as it may seem to outsiders. (If my neighbors saw me dancing with my cat, they never mentioned it. On the other hand, they moved away, so maybe that's all I need to know!)

When *you're* missing the pet you love, please remember that the bond created in life reaches far beyond death. The pets we've loved and lost remain with us in our daily lives. And it is with great certainty that I say that they will greet us with tails wagging, whiskers twitching, squeaks, squawks, and barks when we join them for a dance on the other side of life.

47. Do pets reincarnate?

Beloved pets are often here for what seems like a cruelly short time. As the Western belief in reincarnation has surged, it is understandable to hope that the pet we love will jump back into a body to have another go-around with us.

With that in mind, it is important to address what I think is the true concern behind this question: one of the greatest fears we have is that we might miss a loved one if we don't synchronize our rides on the karmic wheel. In other words, what happens if a pet gets reincarnated somewhere on the other side of the world—perhaps as a sacred cow— and we never meet again?

First, let me reassure you that, from the messages I've received directly from pets, they emphasize that they remain with us in spirit. I have yet to speak with any pet—dog, cat, or otherwise—who says, "I'll be back in six months and waiting for you to pick me up at the Pasadena Humane Society." Instead, during sessions and events, pets in spirit remind those who love them that the length of their life on Earth does not limit their connection to these loved ones. One of the reasons it is important to understand this is so that we aren't looking for a beloved pet where that pet doesn't exist. When it comes to pets, it is connection, cooperation, and contract that are important, rather than tracking life after life for personal growth.

A beloved pet in spirit may also bring you together with the pet that is perfect for your life now. So don't be surprised (as pets in spirit often prompt me to say) if you end up with a Rottweiler even though you've always had pugs. Or if you're a devoted Persian cat lover, you could end up with a Chihuahua. Love comes in many packages—pets in spirit know that. It is up to us to let go of preconceived ideas of how those packages must come wrapped—especially if we assume that the pet we love has been reincarnated.

A memorable meeting with two dog moms and their cocker spaniel in spirit helped clarify the confusion surrounding pet reincarnation. It was the final appointment of the day, and when I opened the door to my office, I came face-to-face with two women: one determined looking and the other looking worried. It was almost as though the appointment had interrupted an ongoing discussion—a discussion that didn't have an easy answer.

Oh boy, I thought.

Actually, what I should have thought was *oh dog*, for as they stepped into my office, I felt a brushing against my lower legs—a sure sign that a midsized dog was accompanying the two sitters.

After the opening prayer, I glanced around the ladies to see which spirits might make an appearance. I saw no one and felt nothing except for the insistent brushing against my leg. I then caught a glimpse of blond, highlighted, wavy hair worthy of Jennifer Aniston. In my ear, I heard the old-time tune, "Oh my darlin' Clementine." When I shared this with the sitters, the one named Marion gasped, and the other, Toni, started to cry.

"Oh, that's Clementine, our cocker spaniel." That was all the permission Clementine needed to launch into the details of her life, which had ended several months before. Oh, to be darlin' Clementine! She had walks, treats, homemade food, a custom bed, and spa treatments. All of that was nice to hear; and she made sure her moms knew how much she appreciated their love for her each and every day.

However, her real reason for visiting was this: "Clementine is showing me a litter of puppies with a big question mark."

The women looked at each other for a brief moment, and Marion said, "I understand that."

"Clementine is showing me one of the puppies with a toy—I think it is *her* toy."

"Yes, I understand that," acknowledged Toni.

"What Clementine is showing me is that she is standing next to the puppy, coaching him how to play with a toy. Clementine tells the puppy, 'If you play with it this way, they [meaning the two women] will like it!"

For a moment, there was silence in the room, from both Clementine and her moms. Then Toni explained, "I really wanted to get another dog, but Marion wasn't so sure. Then, when I met a group of cocker pups, there was one who immediately picked up a toy I brought, which was Clementine's favorite, and played with it just as Clementine did. I thought that maybe Clementine had reincarnated and come back to us."

Marion, after taking a deep breath and letting out a sigh, said, "I'm so relieved. I really wasn't ready for another dog but wouldn't have wanted to turn Clementine away." I don't know whether Toni and Marion adopted the cocker pup, but I do know that they were no longer fearful about losing Clementine *again*.

This kind of thinking isn't as strange as it may seem at first. As Buddhism has moved into the Western world, His Holiness the Dalai Lama's reincarnation story has become well known: after a lama dies, it is typical for priests and other devotees to find his reincarnated spirit by visiting villages until a boy recognizes his personal possessions. But let me remind you that dogs are not lamas (or llamas either!).

Time and again, pets in spirit have demonstrated that they communicate with other pets in the household and "instruct" potential family members. A Tibetan spaniel in spirit told me that she coached a German shepherd puppy at the shelter to tilt her head and raise her eyebrow just as she used to. A tuxedo cat in spirit, who had a particular animus toward birds, tutored a young calico that joined her family to sit in the window and chatter all day long at her feathered "friends." One of my favorite encounters was with a pug named Bear, who was absolutely no nonsense when it came to reining in the over-the-top energy of the family's new Jack Russell terrier. "That's funny," said Bear's mom, in response to the news. "Our new dog will be running around like crazy or digging a hole in the yard, and then suddenly stop and lie down. Guess Bear is babysitting for us." Yes, Bear, Clementine, and all the other beloved pets in spirit are a bit like clones of Cesar Millan (the "Dog Whisperer").

So what does all this say about whether pets do or do not reincarnate? Well, I can only report what I know to be true. And what I know is that pets in spirit are much more interested in reestablishing contact with loved ones than they are in projecting their plans for a future life, or even reviewing past lives. Maybe the most important thing to know for sure is that reincarnation will never keep us from those who love us and those whom we love.

48. Do animals in spirit help us in our lives?

It is now an accepted fact that animals on Earth are of great benefit, whether they are bomb-sniffing dogs or service and support animals. Take my dog, Bodhi, for instance. He has traveled from coast to coast and attended conventions, gallery-style events, workshops, circles, and private sessions. He has licked the tears of a woman whose husband was murdered and comforted a lady who lost her son and mother.

About three years after adopting Bodhi, I found another member of the family named Amara at a rescue organization in Orange County, California. At the first spirit circle Amara attended, she walked up to a lady in the group and looked at her with a gentle demand to be picked up. When the spirits drew me to this woman for messages, in short order, we met her husband, son, and dog in spirit, all of whom had died within months of one another.

I understand that the question is whether animals in spirit help us, but I bring up Bodhi and Amara to make a point: they work on Earth in cooperation with spirits (just like me). When people come to see me, oftentimes the trauma and pain of loss have slammed shut their hearts. If this happens, it can be more difficult for someone to feel the presence of loved ones in spirit. Enter Bodhi and Amara: between their size, personality, and yes, extensive wardrobes, they easily bring out the *aw* reflex in people. Once that happens, the heart begins to soften and open a little bit. Many people have held one of my dogs to their chest, and I could almost see the change—the heart opening, even if just a crack—right before my eyes.

When I'm doing a larger gallery-style event, animals in spirit will often help to organize the order of messages. As you can imagine, the energy (and the numbers of spirits present) at an event with 200+ people is intense. However, animals in spirit help guide me to the person or group of people where I'm to start. Usually, the dogs in spirit are Labrador retrievers or German shepherds—oddly (or not?), the very breeds most often used as guide dogs for the blind. So, I guess that when I ask to be guided, they take the request literally!

This reminds me of a story about a German shepherd I met during a spirit circle. Instead of seeing people in spirit around a young man named Steven, a shepherd in spirit with an "L" name lay at his feet. When I mentioned this, the young man said, "Two weeks ago, I had to put my German shepherd, Luna, to sleep. She was my one and only dog for fourteen years."

Luna went on to communicate that she was not only still around him but also guiding his steps on life's path. Luna had helped Steven learn to walk again after a car accident, and she wasn't about to give up her role as guide and cheerleader. Steven was relieved to learn that having to put Luna down hadn't diminished her love for him.

It isn't only pets in spirit that help us with our lives—*all* animals do. This point was made during a spirit circle in New York: "You are surrounded by animals in spirit," I mentioned to a young woman, who was the first to receive a message in the group. "These are big animals—an elephant, a tiger, and a giraffe. The elephant's trunk is over your shoulder in a kind of hug. The animals are expressing thanks for your work on their behalf."

She took these comments in stride as I went on to speak with her dear friend in spirit who had died from a self-inflicted gunshot wound. The animals, however, remained in place, surrounding her—almost as a protective posse. After the circle, I learned that this woman worked for a cable network devoted to animals. There wasn't any indication that she knew the animals in spirit personally, but they obviously knew who she was and what her work entailed, as well as the grief she was now facing with the loss of her friend.

During a private session, I met another wild animal that, in other circumstances, might have seemed threatening: "There is a wolf in spirit sitting right next to you," I relayed to the man before me. "He isn't moving, just sitting there. He gives me a sense that he helps you with your work."

The wolf went on to provide information about the man's life and relationships. After the session concluded, the sitter smiled and said, "As soon as you saw my wolf companion, I knew you were the real deal. The wolf is always with me and indeed helps me with my work."

I was delighted to learn that the sitter was a well-respected shaman. And from that day forward, I could see and connect with the power animals, which are spirit guides in animal form.

The cooperation, coordination, and connection between animals in spirit and people underscores how we're constantly guided, protected, and helped by them on our journeys. During a spirit circle for volunteers of an animal rescue, I saw a beautiful, strong red horse with a white blaze (a strip of white coloring), standing behind a woman who was well put together, from head to toe. As I described the horse, she nodded in recognition. The horse went on to share that as much as this woman had wanted to ride as a young girl, her parents wouldn't allow it for fear that she would be injured. After school, the girl would tell all her worldly troubles to the red horse in a neighbor's paddock. And now, as the woman faced challenges and difficulties in her life, including the end of a lengthy marriage, the horse said, "When it seems as though you can walk no further, let me carry you."

Animals in spirit aren't shy about declaring their ongoing commitment to us as the following encounter demonstrates: "There's a German shepherd sitting by your side," I said to a man attending an event with his wife. I had the feeling that he wasn't entirely open to the experience of spirit communication, since his arms were firmly crossed over his chest. "The dog gives me the feeling that he is your partner."

With that statement, the man raised one of his hands to his face to cover his eyes. The dog continued to give me information about their life together, including finding his "toy" (which actually meant hidden illegal drugs) and his favorite treat (hot dogs). At one point, the dog placed his paw on the thigh of the man, who was a retired drug-enforcement officer. When I relayed this bit of information, the man dropped his hands to his lap and told me that on the day the dog had to be put down, his last action was to place his paw on the man's knee. Although the dog had received commendations for his lifetime of service, after dying, he offered his undying friendship . . . and love.

The loving animals in our lives, on Earth and in spirit, do indeed carry us and remain our partners—animals are our guides as much as, if not more than, we are their caretakers. These important relationships survive death and can be fostered through spirit communication. The love between humans and animals continues to grow beyond the earthly plane, into eternity.

Animals in spirit may not be sniffing out bombs, but they *can* alert us to danger. Animals in spirit may not be guiding the blind, but they *can* guide a medium to those blinded by grief. Animals in spirit may not be able to provide hands-on emotional support, but they *can* bring us to the places, people, and pets that can.

So yes, animals in spirit can and *do* help us in our lives—and probably far more than we know.

> *For more on animal guides, read Q&A number 36,*
> *"What is the difference between guides and angels?" in chapter 5,*
> *"Afterlife Relationships."*

8

Spirited Occasions

49. Do spirits honor holiday traditions?

Tradition is defined as "something that is handed down" or "a long-established or inherited way of thinking and acting." An eleven-year-old boy in spirit named Steven demonstrated that he knew the meaning of tradition. During a session scheduled two weeks before Christmas, he showed me a vision of a Christmas tree decked with homemade ornaments. His mother confirmed that every year, their family would choose and bring home a live tree, then make ornaments to decorate it. They had been doing this for so many years (eleven, to be exact), that the tree was covered with ornaments that the parents and their son had created together.

At the time of our session, Steven's mother was debating whether or not to continue the tradition. The idea of setting up the tree without her son sharing in the fun was too painful for her to consider. However, when her son dropped the idea of a living tree with roots into my head, she responded, "Well, we thought about planting a pine tree in our yard in memory of our son. Maybe that's what we should do."

Shortly after Christmas, I received a photo of the chosen tree planted in the backyard. It was festooned with homemade ornaments, and orbs and mist appeared between the branches, even obscuring some of them. (Orbs, which look like bubbles, indicate a spirit presence in both digital and film photographs. Unexplained mist and streaks of light may be spirits moving quickly through the frame of a photo.)

I have no doubt that Steven wanted to inspire his parents to celebrate the holiday in a new and life-affirming way. In doing so, the entire family honored the evolution of the tradition, with Steven demonstrating his participation by showing up in the photos.

Traditional holiday fare is another hot topic with spirits. Grandmothers in spirit will mention recipes that their grandchildren are trying to duplicate. A father in spirit gave me a taste of the pasta that he made from scratch every Christmas. He also showed me a holiday table laden with pasta and two kinds of meat. His daughters now make "his" pasta with his grandchildren, and they set a place for him at their holiday table. Spirits don't need the physical nourishment, of course, but they enjoy participating in the preparation and serving of holiday dinners.

One family told me that the candles on their table furiously burned down to nothing in less than a minute the first Christmas after their mother had passed. It was a family tradition that the candles be lit only when the entire family was gathered at the table. This mother in spirit made sure her family knew that she was present as well. You know the old saying "I'll be with you in spirit"? Spirits take that literally!

Loved ones in spirit know that holiday traditions—whether its celebrating Easter, Christmas, Passover, Ramadan, Halloween, and so forth—provide a sense of continuity from generation to generation. Therefore, it shouldn't be surprising that spirits honor our traditions and continue to join in with their presence and their love. But as is so often the case, the presence of spirits can transform traditions and limited ways of thinking into a celebration of their lives and opportunities for communication.

One American holiday in which tradition takes center stage is Thanksgiving, a time when family and friends gather. Although the holiday isn't celebrated specifically with spirits in mind, clients over the years have asked how to include loved ones who have passed. In fact, Thanksgiving provides the perfect opportunity to honor loved ones in spirit and offer our gratitude to them.

Listening to many spirit messages about holidays, food, and family has provided the following template for celebrating (Thanksgiving or any other holiday) with loved ones in spirit. And of course, each person and every family is welcome to adapt these suggestions to suit their particular situation.

Celebrate by giving thanks for the life of your loved one.

Now, this might seem an obvious point when it is Thanksgiving, but a loved one's death can make us feel anything *but* grateful around holidays. However, I've learned from spirits that gratitude paves the way for connection. One of the simplest ways of giving thanks is to sit quietly and thank the person in spirit directly. Thank a brother for his great sense of humor or a friend for her support during difficult times. These experiences we've shared on Earth can never be taken from us, even by death.

Celebrate by remembering the good times.

It is natural during holiday celebrations to reminisce about previous family gatherings. During a phone session on Thanksgiving Eve, a father in spirit flashed a picture into my mind of a dog with a turkey leg in its mouth. The wife and daughter on the other end of the phone laughed while trying to explain that he had dropped the turkey on the floor one Thanksgiving Day, and their dog, Lady, had dragged it off in her mouth. Loved ones in spirit remember the good times too, and they laugh with us in the reminiscing.

Celebrate by enjoying a favorite activity.

During a phone session, there was a young man who mentioned Hawaii and surfing. His mother acknowledged that they went to Hawaii every Thanksgiving week and that her son was a major surfer. Though she and her husband couldn't bear taking the trip the year their son died, they were thinking of returning. Her son in spirit demonstrated his enthusiasm for the idea by making the phone line crackle. There was more crackling when his mother mentioned that she wanted to take a surfing lesson. Loved ones in spirit share our new experiences and want to cheer us on.

Celebrate by cooking a favorite family recipe or going out to a restaurant that a loved one enjoyed.

In nearly every session, food is mentioned. This is not because spirits need it for their nourishment; it's because celebrations, family, friends, and food go together. Plus, a home-cooked meal has become an iconic idea. At a November event one year, a grandmother in spirit mentioned her granddaughter's efforts to re-create her family's favorite five-spice cake. Unfortunately, this grandmother hadn't written down the recipe, but she wanted her granddaughter to know that she was helping her in the kitchen.

Celebrate by becoming more aware.

We can celebrate any holiday by becoming more aware of how loved ones may be communicating with us directly. This awareness may begin by spending a few minutes each day with a quieted mind and an attitude of gratitude. By including your loved ones in spirit in your holiday traditions (and all your celebrations), you're inviting them to remain connected and to guide you with their love.

50. Do the holidays draw spirits closer to us?

In thousands—maybe even millions—of messages I've received from spirits, they have demonstrated that they participate in the celebrations of our lives. That being said, designated holidays don't have a special pull; it's the love-filled gathering of families and friends that raises the energy spirits can use to make their presence known. To encourage your awareness of loved ones in spirit during special times of the year, here are a few suggestions for including spirits in your celebrations, both big and small.

Decorate.

Many of us already have areas in our homes that help us feel closer to those we love in spirit: a mantel with family photos; a nightstand with a beloved picture; a room with stuffed animals on the bed, where a young person used to sleep. Adding decorative flourishes during the holidays—especially the kind your loved ones enjoyed while on Earth—doesn't go unnoticed by those in spirit.

During a private session, a son in spirit named Lee asked his parents to hang lights all over the house for Christmas. "Be sure that Santa is on the roof!" I reminded Lee's parents, as Lee showed me a vision of Santa, reindeer and all. Lee's father confirmed that every year, each house in the neighborhood would compete for the best display of lights and lighted figures. "Santa and the reindeer was the last big decoration we bought before Lee died. I didn't know if I could bring myself to put it up on the roof this year."

Shortly after the New Year, Lee's dad contacted me to say that the best thing he did was to honor his son's wishes. Many of the neighbors made comments like, "Lee would love it," and Lee's father felt his son's presence with every expression of delight.

Eat.

Spirits talk about food—*a lot*. It seems as though they never miss a meal that we make with them in mind. If you cook it, bake it, or make it, they will come. In return, those in spirit may give you the smells of their favorite recipes when there is nothing in the oven. A woman who came to see me thought she was going crazy, because she constantly smelled the scent of barbecued ribs; since her husband's death, she hadn't even fired up the grill. She was surprised and delighted when her husband brought up in our session that he was busy making his secret recipe for barbecued ribs.

Sing.

Loved ones in spirit love music, especially the music they loved on Earth. So, turn up the tunes and share their music! I've heard church music, rap, metal, old rock 'n' roll, big band, and accordion music during times of spirit connection. One mother got a shock (and a thrill) when she got in her car to come see me, turned on the radio, and instead of hearing classical music, rap came blaring out! Before her son died, the two of them would argue about which station to listen to while driving. She was happy to let him win the argument this time!

Remember.

Spirits love to remember the good times, and they want you to as well. Sometimes, the last memory we have of someone we love is the dying scene at the hospital or the harsh words said shortly before a car accident or suicide. During sessions, spirits don't spend a lot of time on those memories; they like to remember the happy times, especially holiday times. A husband in spirit thanked his wife for all the delicious dinners she cooked on Christmas Day. He loved the meat (always a ham *and* a turkey) and the homemade gnocchi. Those in spirit also like to remember and share family jokes.

Those in spirit will often comment on weddings, reunions, and parties that took place before *and* after they died. So, keep making new memories; those you love in spirit don't miss these occasions.

Forgive.

One of the most significant and profound ways to bring those in spirit close to you is to forgive them for dying and leaving you behind. This may seem too much to ask, but releasing the anguish, anger, and guilt about a loved one's passing is like dismantling the wall we've built, brick by brick, between life and death. When you ask to feel a loved one near, consider the following words of forgiveness: "*I forgive you* for not taking care of yourself the way you should have so that your life could have been longer. *I forgive you* for not beating the addiction that took you so young. *I forgive you* for choosing to end your own life, and *I forgive myself* for not preventing it. *I forgive*

you for _____ , and *I forgive myself* for
_____ ." Just fill in the blanks in whatever
way applies to the circumstances.

Forgiveness allows love to flourish and diminishes feelings of
separation. Know that those you love will hear you and draw close,
for the celebrations of life, like birthdays, holidays, and everyday
life too.

* * *

Do the holidays bring our loved ones to us automatically? No. But the
love we've shared and continue to share during these special celebrations keeps them close to us during the holidays—and *always*.

51. How can I manage during the holidays when missing someone I love?

This question reminds me of the time I woke up suddenly with an
anxious feeling that continued to grow until it was bordering on
panic. I couldn't quite catch my breath; the clock said it was 6:33 AM.

As a psychic medium, I know that I am affected by the energy
of the planet and have a sense when a momentous event or shift is
about to happen (like 9/11 in 2001 and the stock market meltdown of
2008). Despite the grounding and protection practices I employ on a

daily basis, I can still be affected by the emotions and states of mind of those who are around me, just like anyone else.

Whenever I'm overwhelmed emotionally or energetically, the first thing I do is *pause*. . . . This provides space for exploring what is going on without reacting to it. In that quiet space, I can check in with myself to see if the energies I am picking up are public or personal, and determine what action may be required. Discerning whether the "threat" is public or not is often as simple as observing how the energy is affecting my body.

Personal concerns tend to have a heart resonance akin to the warmth we feel when thinking of someone we love. Once I discern where the energy is hitting me, it is easier to ascertain whether I'm connected to the public network of Earth or the private network of family and friends. This process is similar to when my computer asks if a new network I'm signing on to should be considered "home" or "public." On the morning I awoke with that extreme anxiety, I discerned that the network to which I was connecting was a home network (not public), so then I had to determine whether or not someone close to me was in danger or if something else was going on.

It was then that I saw my cousin Tommy (in spirit) standing next the bed—and it hit me: *Thanksgiving*. My dear cousin had killed himself at the age of nineteen on Thanksgiving Eve many years ago. Standing next to him was his mother, my auntie Sue in spirit, who had died just a few months prior. This was their first Thanksgiving in the afterlife together. The evening before this visitation, I had ordered my Thanksgiving dinner. Coincidence? Absolutely not.

Despite my being a medium and despite Tommy having died years ago, Thanksgiving still brings anxiety—the sense that something is about to happen—even when I'm not thinking about it consciously. Tommy's presence in spirit didn't bring the anxiety; it was related to my own feelings about what had happened years ago. His and auntie

Sue's presence actually brought—and still brings—an antidote of clarity and peace.

Grief and trauma—and the anxiety associated with them—are sneaky. It doesn't matter how long ago a loved one passed; holidays can still be tough. For this reason, I'd like to share with you some ways to manage the anxiety that the holidays can activate.

Breathe.

Many times, a few minutes of paying attention to your breathing—in and out—can calm anxiety before it builds out of control. This simple practice also brings us into the present moment so that we're less focused on what has happened in the past (which we might want to change) or what could happen in the future (something we cannot know for certain). It can also provide the necessary pause to begin to discern where the emotional overload is coming from.

Be in your body.

Sit upright in a chair, with your feet flat on the floor. If you start to panic or cry in a public space, just stop for a moment and imagine the soles of your feet attached to the floor with magnets. Don't worry about the other people—they'll walk around you. This is a simple yet effective way to get instantly grounded.

Create a memory box.

You can purchase an embellished box or decorate an everyday shoebox yourself (if you're crafty). Each day during the holiday season, write down a happy memory on a slip of paper and add it to the box. Do not be surprised if your loved ones in spirit inspire you to remember funny moments. (They like laughter.)

Share memories.

Take time to share memories of loved ones in spirit with friends and family. If there are new family members (those just married in or born), include them in the stories. And take plenty of photos—loved ones in spirit may show up as orbs, streaks of light, or mist.

Express gratitude.

Make a statement of gratitude aloud in the evening or in the morning, or keep a gratitude journal. Living in an attitude of gratitude is the simplest way to create a bridge to loved ones in spirit and to relieve anxiety during the holidays or any day.

$$* * *$$

One last thing to mention is that there aren't calendars in the afterlife, nor do spirits have notifications that pop up on their phones when a holiday is near. However, if we're thinking about loved ones in spirit on a particular holiday and are including them in our celebrations, it's like sending a huge message of love to them. They get it!

By creating space between the pressures of the holidays and the anxiety they bring, we're inviting loved ones in spirit into our experience of the present. With their help, we can manage and may even enjoy the holidays once again.

9

The Big Questions

52. Do spirits tell you if there's a God?

Yes! But it is more accurate to state that spirits tell me about *their* version of God.

"I want to die and see the face of God"—these were the dying words a loving mother in spirit gave me to share with her daughter. And her words were so intriguing that, of course, I had to ask: "And did you?"

"I didn't see God's face," the mother said, "but God is everywhere!!"

Sometimes, spirits provide a full line of thought, as in this case. I'm always grateful for that because, as a medium, when it comes to God, you want to get it right!

I have communicated with spirits and people who are Christian, Jewish, Hindu, Muslim, Buddhist, atheist, agnostic, and everything in between. As a medium, I see it as my job to be the Switzerland of religion: neutral—I simply report what I see, hear, feel, smell, and taste. What this allows me to do is be accessible to people and spirits without judgment or a demanding allegiance to a belief. What I've discovered is that when I'm connected in love, the gods that people relate to and recognize show up with them. But sometimes even I'm surprised.

During a trip to Egypt in 2019, I was with a group that was privileged to have an opportunity to meditate in a small room with a statue of the Egyptian goddess Sekhmet, which was thousands of years old. Away from the crowds, we waited in great anticipation as one member of our group, a dear friend of mine, unlocked a large wooden door and walked through to an inner chamber. What I heard next was wailing—it was my friend. Not sure exactly what I'd find as I stepped gingerly into the chamber, I saw my friend at the base of the statue, suddenly calm. The group and I gathered around her, people closed their eyes, and a meditation began. I, however, didn't close my eyes. Perhaps it is the teacher in me, needing to monitor a group, but it is usually my habit to watch what's going on during a group meditation. Rather than looking around at the others in the room, my gaze was riveted to the statue. As the meditation continued, the head of the statue began to sway side to side. I blinked, not quite believing what my eyes were showing me. The meditation continued, and I became alarmed when it seemed as though the statue, rocking forward and backward now, was going to tumble onto the group. As suddenly as the rocking began, however, it stopped. I decided to say nothing about what I saw until I could make more sense of it.

Following the meditation, I learned that my friend had previously connected with this goddess Sekhmet during a difficult time. She credited Sekhmet with freeing her from negative influences in her life. (In case you're not familiar with Egyptian deities, Sekhmet is a warrior goddess and a goddess of healing.)

As we were leaving the temple, I overheard the youngest person who had come on the trip say, to no one in particular, "I thought I saw the statue moving in there . . ."

Indeed. Sometimes even a medium needs validation that something really happened. And on that day, in that temple, God was a Goddess.

In another situation, the evidence for the existence of God wasn't made nearly as clear. It was Christmastime, so it makes sense that God was on the minds of the two spirits standing behind a woman who was comfortably seated in my office. She was wearing a green sweater with a little angel pin. Both spirits gave me the feeling of a father, so I said to the woman, "I have two male spirits here, both fathers. As I look at them, they seem to be in a bit of a face-off." (They weren't looking directly at me but at each other.) And then I overheard the strangest conversation: "There is a God," said one. "There is no God," said the other.

When I reported this exchange to the sitter, she laughed—an unexpected response. "Oh, that's my father and father-in-law having the same argument they had at every Christmas dinner!" she declared. For her, the conversation wasn't about God; instead, it meant that her father and father-in-law, both of whom she loved, were together in the afterlife. For her, their conversation was evidence of them surviving death and being together, not whether God existed or not.

And really, wouldn't their deaths finally settle that argument? That was the question I went home with that night. As I thought about God, I was reminded of the miracles I saw during my time as a Christian singer. As I sang songs about God and a personal relationship with God, I begin to see spirits standing with people in the pews. These spirits were grandmothers and grandfathers, fathers and fathers-in-law, friends, and others. It was then that I began to share the love of these spirits with people as well. It seemed to me that God and heaven (as I used to call the afterlife) might be far more mysterious and amazing than I could conceive. And in that moment, inspired by that original question, I became a mystic—one no longer willing to define God but to experience all that the spirit world was willing to share with me.

The lyrics to the chorus of one of the last Christian songs I wrote reflects my changing views:

> You are a God of the unexpected,
> The daily-miracle kind.
> Forgive me for trying to contain You
> Within the confines of my mind.

As a medium, I can't prove to you that God exists, just as I can't prove to you that spirits exist. I'm not asking you to have faith, either;

I just ask that you be willing to consider the evidence as it is presented. Ultimately, I encourage you to have your own experiences with spirits and your Higher Power, whatever shape that Higher Power may take.

> *For more on how mediums connect with iconic spiritual figures, read Q&A number 11, "Do religious figures such as Mother Mary and Jesus communicate through mediums?" in chapter 2, "On Being a Medium."*

53. What does it mean to be spiritually connected?

Being spiritually connected means being plugged into a network of spirits, some of whom we knew personally, in physical form, and some of whom we are introduced to and grow in relationship with as we walk a chosen spiritual path. In other words, we can continue relationships with family members and pets who have died, while also developing relationships with guides, angels, and gods/goddesses.

It is a natural—*not* supernatural—thing to be spiritually connected, whether we're actively pursuing those links or not. Humans are essentially spirit beings living as physical beings; how each of us explores and expands that natural spiritual connection is a personal choice. And that choice can be greatly influenced by community/culture, religious upbringing, education, and travel. For example, with the influx of Eastern mystical beliefs and customs during the

1960s and 1970s, meditation and yoga followed, becoming an everyday part of our American culture and general wellness practices.

As a medium, I've been privileged to introduce people to their spirit networks, which may include family members they didn't even know. These days, it isn't unusual to see ancestors who were deeply religious surrounding a person on Earth who identifies as spiritual. Interestingly enough, these ancestors intimate that it is their devotion to religion and God that has laid the groundwork for spiritual awareness into the DNA of the family.

It is also possible to be spiritually connected to others, including nonhumans, living on Earth. If you've considered reincarnation as a possibility, that belief could explain the evident frisson when you meet someone and feel as though you know that person. The spiritual connection we share with others on Earth is demonstrated by psychic "hits" we receive when something is wrong with a loved one living miles away. When we're really in tune with someone, we can even experience a kind of intuitive synchronicity. For example, while driving with a boyfriend on the 101 freeway in California, I turned to him and said, "Yes, let's stop for lunch if we have time." Shocked, he told me that he had been wondering whether we should stop for lunch. I thought I was responding to something he had said aloud!

Spirits can use our connection to one another to reinforce their connection with us. In other words, spirits may use others in your earthly network to communicate with you. For instance, a friend who went to see a medium received messages from *my* mother in spirit. (Apparently, I wasn't listening!) Another friend of mine was surprised when a coworker called him "Pumpkin." The coworker was shocked and couldn't explain why she felt compelled to do such a thing. Interestingly, my friend's grandmother had died a few days earlier, and she used to call him "Pumpkin"!

Being spiritually connected also means being an open and available conduit for messages that support our collective healing, wellness, and growth. This is underscored by the frequency of angel encounters. Not long ago, during a session, a young woman in spirit stood with the angels who had appeared in her hospital room right before she died. "Dying was easy. I flew on the wings of angels," she declared. Her aunt confirmed that she had prayed for the angels to come for her niece. In general, I've been receiving more and more reports of angel encounters from clients and workshop participants. Fortunately, there are a lot of people listening and sharing the divine messages they bring.

The desire to be consciously and spiritually connected is expanding exponentially. We're waking up to the idea that being spiritually connected creates a fulfilling and guided life; that being spiritually connected gives us a sense of being an essential part of the greater whole; that being spiritually connected allows for the greatest expression of the Golden Rule (do unto others as you would have them do unto you). We're learning that being spiritually connected isn't a denial of the physical but an opportunity to bring spiritual awareness and expansiveness into the physical.

Recently, in one week alone, I communicated with a young man who died when hit by a train, a boy of twelve who was hit and killed while riding a bicycle, a man of twenty who died by suicide, and another who died after mixing drugs and alcohol. Their families and friends got in touch with me to reconnect with their loved ones, to feel their presence again. Being spiritually connected destroys the illusion that we are separate and alone, and it's something we all have access to.

So, what does it mean to be spiritually connected? It means that we never lose the people we love.

For more on angels, read Q&A number 36, "What is the difference between guides and angels?" in chapter 5, "Afterlife Relationships."

54. Is it true that our experiences on Earth are a sort of life school?

You've probably heard references to the "school of life" and may have assumed that this school is only Earth based—that spirits live beyond its curriculum. Not so. For spirits, school's not out for summer *or* for eternity.

For example, during a recent spirit circle, a father in spirit expressed remorse for the years on Earth that he'd spent drinking. "I didn't know how to be a loving father," he told his son, who had come to see me. He went on to say, "I'm watching you raise your own son, and I've learned so much from you." His son acknowledged that he was devoting his life and time to raising his son differently from the way he had been raised. Imagine that—a father in spirit learning how to be a father from his own son on Earth.

Because I've been doing the work of spirit communication for years, I've had the opportunity to speak with the same spirits a number of times. Sometimes, it is like meeting up with an old friend and witnessing the changes that life experience brings. As a result of repeated meetings, spirits have shown me that growing and changing continues after death.

This truth is underscored by a visit with a teenage girl in spirit (with whom I'd had many conversations) who recounted her experience with mental illness, which had resulted in her taking her own life. She didn't present me with a list of grievances or place blame for her situation; instead, a sense of peace fell over the room as I spoke with her—a peace unlike what her mother and I had felt during earlier readings.

"Where did this begin?" I asked her (in my mind, in reference to the changes she experienced after her death).

In answering, she brought forward other spirits in her family line who had helped her make sense of what she experienced here on Earth. The other spirits included her grandmother; her father, who had suffered a similar mental illness that wrenched the family apart; and the grandfather who was a source of pain in the family due to neglect and abuse. These people (some of whom she had known on Earth and others she hadn't) had impacted her life before death and in the afterlife. The end result was that she learned where her illness began, bringing understanding and compassionate insight to her life experience. Enlightenment came quietly and in peace; and it was so powerful that her mother and I could feel it here on Earth. Her mother expressed it perfectly by saying, "This session makes everything feel complete somehow."

After talking with the young woman in spirit, I asked the spirits to help clarify the differences between the school of life on Earth and the learning process after death. The answer to my questions came in the form of a vision—a vision of a jigsaw puzzle.

The spirits showed me a table on which puzzle pieces, which were all jumbled at first, began to separate from one another. Some moved from the center pile and were labeled "gravity," "time," "birth," "decay," and "death." Other pieces filled in the border, and I had the sense that they represented beliefs about how the world works and the judgments made about ourselves, others, and even God. It hadn't occurred to me that beliefs and judgments are just as real as gravity, adding to the earthly limitations we live within.

At this point, the jigsaw puzzle in the vision became a thick and, in some places, impermeable border. Within that firm border, pieces labeled "experiences" began to bring color and shape to the picture inside. Pieces representing people I know and love, along with pieces representing people who have hurt me deeply—all these pieces fit together to create the picture of my life. In a flash of insight, I got that what I've learned about life, the physical world, and my interior worlds was part of the picture within the borders as well.

However, in my vision, the jigsaw puzzle wasn't finished; and this caused me a bit of consternation because I prefer visions to be clear (which isn't always the case). I then heard the word *death*, and the puzzle's border began disappearing, piece by piece. I noticed that it happened gradually rather than all at once. Eventually, only the center jumble of pieces remained, partially put together. It occurred to me at this point that enlightenment may not come all at once with death, as I would like to believe.

As I sat and waited, I noticed that the interior puzzle pieces began to join with other pieces that I hadn't seen before. The pieces matched up perfectly and completely, and kept getting bigger and bigger— literally becoming "the big picture." *Wow—everything and everyone connecting to create a whole . . .*

I understand that this "big picture" concept isn't new; however, spirits hadn't presented it to me in such a simple yet dramatic way before. Then it occurred to me that what I had seen was a pictorial representation of how the limitations of the physical world—our beliefs and judgments—actually separate the interior pieces of our puzzle from connecting to the biggest picture. In essence, what I was seeing was what we, on Earth, aspire to yet may not really grasp: complete understanding through expansion and connection.

After dying, all the questions we have here on Earth—questions like *Why did this have to happen? What could I have done better? Where did it begin?*—are answered. They may not be answered before death simply because we're missing pieces of the puzzle, or because we're unwilling to let go of limiting judgments and beliefs. As a medium, I know that spirits give me information in ways that our brains can process. But there is *so much more* to life in spirit than I'm allowed to see or can understand in my physical form.

While writing this, I remembered a session with a gentleman who has actively pursued a spiritual life here on Earth. His wife, now in spirit, was also on a spiritual quest before her death. In speaking with her numerous times since her passing, it has been made clear that her quest to know and understand hasn't diminished one bit. During our last session together, she gave a description of the place (or space) to which we're all heading. Here are some of the words and phrases she used: "A place that transcends life and death . . . where no separation exists . . . where *All* is a state of being . . . returning to God." She then added a phrase that was startling in its profundity—she called it "the place of no fragments."

The place of no fragments: a place where everything fits together, where it all makes sense, where we not only see the big picture but are also an integral part of it. It sounds as though this "oneness" is what spirits want to share with us—one puzzle piece at a time. But the point is: we're always growing and changing, and we're always connected.

55. Do spirits agree with us about what is good and what is bad?

In answering this question, I was tempted to launch into a discussion of justice from the spirits' point of view. However, I dealt with the idea of justice in my previous book, *I'm Not Dead, I'm Different*. Although bound to repeat myself when discussing important topics, I thought it best to explore good and bad from another angle altogether. This answer begins, as many do, with a story.

During the summer, I visited another place in another time. No, I'm not talking about a quantum physics or time-travel moment but a day spent at the Renaissance Pleasure Faire in Irwindale, California. Late in the day, I overheard a man in a doublet say to another dressed similarly, "I love watching the weird people walk by." I followed his gaze—he was looking at a mother, father, and two kids dressed in shorts, T-shirts, and baseball caps. Weird? Well, only if you are a duke living in the 1500s (or have chosen to believe you are). I guffawed (inwardly, of course) because I, too, was dressed in a T-shirt, jeans, and sneakers.

Driving home in the car, I was hit by the thought that our frame of reference, coupled with our beliefs about what we perceive, results in our making judgments about the nature of reality (good or bad). This equation can simply be stated: *Perspective + Belief = Judgment.*

Though it may be true that judgment used in the sense of discernment can be positive (as in "using good judgment"), it can also lead to endless suffering if either perspective or belief is limited or in error. In my work as a medium, spirits make it their top priority to correct, or at least reframe, what we've convinced ourselves is true. These messages of love, hope, and healing are the antidotes to judgments made about life, death, love, and how we may have failed those we love—or ourselves.

To illustrate how this works, here's an example:

A male spirit appeared behind a young man at one of my events. At first, the young man in the audience didn't want to acknowledge the spirit, who claimed to be his father. The spirit said that the young man had his name tattooed on his body (which he did). Although his father had died young and the young man never knew him, we learned that he was aware of his son's specific struggles regarding education, a change in career, personal addictions, and family challenges. Imagine that—an unknown father making it clear that he was present throughout his son's life! It took a minute for all of this to sink in.

When this father also thanked his son for making him proud, there wasn't a dry eye in the house. Any judgments that this young man had made around the idea of being fatherless were shifted.

Judgments made as to whether a death is a good or a bad one can have an impact that lasts a lifetime and even generations. Maybe this is most true when it comes to suicide. From the spirits' perspective, things aren't always what they seem, especially as it relates to the dying process. This is a point made clear by a young man in spirit named Matt, who had taken his life in the barn that housed his mother's beloved horses.

His desperate and bereaved mother had considered the barn to be a sacred place—until her son chose to die there. As Matt showed me the place of his death, I could smell hay and heard the comforting sounds of the horses. While I was entranced by the loveliness of the place, he said, "I felt safe with the horses, and that's why I chose to die among them." Both he and I were grateful for the opportunity to present his mother with the truth about his death. For years, she had lived with the idea that her son was angry with her and had chosen to kill himself in a way designed to inflict maximum damage. She thought she had failed her son and that he was punishing her. What she learned instead was that her sacred place was special to him as well. In that moment, what had been profaned became sacred once again.

In a situation like this, the spirit isn't being nice to spare our feelings; spirit communication doesn't work that way. In fact, the truth spirits present is refreshingly free from "spin." I would even suggest that this truth is bigger than our ideas of what is right or wrong. In other words, we can't know whether spirits agree with our assessment about reality unless we're open to their perspective.

In thinking about this, I'm compelled to question my own limited views, which gets expressed in daily frustrations. While driving I've been known to say aloud—quite loudly, in fact—"Why did you have to pull out *right* in front of me?" That same person invariably drops speed and crawls along "just to spite me." In my mind, I give out tickets all day long. (Sigh.) Inviting spirits into the mix might change my perspective (and lower my blood pressure). What if, when I hear a judgment run through my head, I stop and pay attention? What do I believe is causing such a judgment to persist? How might spirits view my situation? By asking these questions rather than determining whether things or people are right or wrong, good or bad, there's the possibility of adding the perspective of spirits, and ultimately, changing the equation of judgment.

One small change in perspective or belief or both can begin to change the way we judge ourselves—and one another. And in the judgment of spirits, that's good.

> *For more on spirits and suicide, read Q&A number 21, "What happens to people who commit suicide?" in chapter 3, "The Dying Experience."*

56. Are soul mates a real thing?

The idea of soul mates has been around for a long time. The only reason I mention this is because, when people ask me about soul mates, there is the expressed assumption that this is a recent, "new age" metaphysical concept. Not so. The genesis of soul mates makes an appearance in Plato's *The Symposium*, with a story about humans being physically split in half. Since that time, the definition of soul mates has evolved. For example, Theosophy, a religious movement that rose to popularity in the late nineteenth century, suggests that God created androgynous souls, which split into genders reuniting when all karma was paid.

These days, however, most people consider a soul mate to be their one-and-only true love. Somewhere along the way, an ancient and somewhat violent cleaving of humankind, along with a loss of the full and completed self, has become the embodiment of "Someday, My Prince Will Come"! Again, not so. Soul mates are *much* more than a romantic fantasy. Spirits have made that clear to me.

The way spirits address the issue of soul mates might be different from what you expect. I hear a lot of other things in the course of my work: names, revving of engines (often signifying a love of motor-cycles), barking, music, and on and on. Not once, however, has a spirit introduced him- or herself as a soul mate. This might be a shocking statement, especially if you consider a loved one in spirit to be *your* soul mate! But don't panic.

Just because I don't hear spirits say "soul mate," doesn't diminish the fact that loved ones in spirit (and we on Earth) share deep, everlasting connections. It may simply be that the term *soul mate* is overused and has therefore lost meaning. It may also be that one term is too limited to encompass the importance of this kind of relationship.

The reason I have come to this conclusion is because of the way that spirits have communicated lifetime and (perhaps) lifetime-through-lifetime connections. Spirits show me brackets—yes, *brackets*. (It is important to point out that this symbol is part of the lexicon I've developed with spirits but not a symbol that is standard for all communicators.) Let me explain how spirits use brackets by sharing a story of two women I met at a spirit circle.

Gwen and Karine dashed into a small spirit circle at the last minute due to a traffic snarl. There weren't two seats together, so they ended up sitting across the room from each other. As I started providing messages for those in attendance, I kept being distracted by a link of light from the top of Gwen's head that crossed the room and ended at the top of Karine's head. No one else in the room had such a link of light. It was as though someone had taken a lighted pen and drawn a bracket connecting their heads!

As it came time to speak with Gwen, the bracket grew even brighter and started to pulse. It was so bright that I glanced around the room to see if anyone else was noticing. My heart started to expand, and I felt a sisterly love but didn't hear the word *sister*. One of my deals with spirits is that I give what I get and don't add to it. I looked at Gwen, pointed to Karine, and said, "You feel like sisters. There's a bracket over your heads signifying that this is a solid connection. Have you considered that you knew each other in a lifetime before this one?"

Gwen laughed and said, "We always joke about being sisters in a former life. We're closer to each other than we are to our own blood families."

Well, members of Gwen's blood family in spirit were standing with her when she said this, and no, they didn't look insulted! Instead, a female spirit, who identified herself as "mother," held up a baby and said "twin." When I relayed this information to Gwen, her mouth dropped open. She was born a twin, but her twin had died. It had been a girl—Gwen's sister. As Gwen's mother continued to provide messages, it became clear that Gwen had spent most of her life looking for a lost sister, whom she had found in Karine.

Let me be clear here that Gwen's mother was not leading me to believe that Karine was actually the lost twin who had reincarnated. Rather, she and the spirit of the twin were together, supporting Gwen, and leading her to Karine through a series of unlikely circumstances. These "coincidences" included Gwen getting locked out of her house at the exact moment that Karine took a "wrong" turn and got a flat tire in front of Gwen's apartment. All of this might seem odd, but the best was yet to come.

Karine had no family members in spirit with her, which I found odd. Instead, a shining being, who felt like a guide, projected a short little movie in my head, showing two little girls playing near the ocean. A large wave crashed to shore, and one little girl ran to shore while the other was swept out to sea. When I described this tragic movie clip to Karine, she gasped. She had experienced a past-life regression the weekend before in which she experienced a similar lifetime. In this past life, she had lost her sister and had spent the rest of her life grieving. She believed she had found that sister in Gwen.

"What?!" exclaimed Gwen. "When were you going to tell me this?"

Karine explained that she had been trying to figure out a way to share the info without it sounding weird. Until that moment, when her guide (the same guide who had been with her during the regression) showed the same info to me, Karine wasn't even sure that she believed it herself. When Gwen confessed to an unreasonable terror of drowning (she was born into a family of swimmers), the group erupted into laughter. The two sisters had found each other!

As this encounter suggests, a soul mate may feel like family, without a romantic element, and family in spirit may bring soul mates together. And the brackets I see, which indicate a deep soul-to-soul connection, can show up at unexpected times, as the next encounter demonstrates.

A client named Kevin, who saw me annually, sat down across from me, and I immediately saw a man in spirit with him who identified himself as "uncle." "My uncle just passed," Kevin confirmed. "In fact, he passed about six months ago." (As an aside, please note that although I may see a client more than once, it is typical for spirits to comment on things happening currently. In addition, there may be different spirits providing messages, depending on the topics being discussed.)

Kevin's uncle didn't allow time for any reaction to this news, but instead took me on a visual tour of Ireland. In my mind, I saw people in traditional dress, smelled Guinness, heard fiddle music, and then saw a castle near a body of water. As I sat entranced by the sight, I could hear the sounds of the water and the lowing of cows. As I described the scene to Kevin, he nodded thoughtfully, as though the scene wasn't nearly as random as it seemed to me.

"This looks like the Dingle Peninsula," I added boldly. (I had visited there while traveling to a friend's wedding. Spirits are good at conveying locations to me, sometimes by name or by highlighting a location on a map they project into my mind, or by reminding me of a place I've been.)

"I just got back from Ireland, and I visited the Dingle Peninsula," Kevin confirmed.

His uncle gave me a feeling of home—a warm settled feeling, a feeling of belonging—as he showed me the castle again. When I shared this feeling with Kevin, he suddenly became emotional.

He cleared his throat and replied, "When I visited the castle ruins on Kilmurry Bay, I immediately felt at home—it was all so familiar."

And then it happened: I saw links! But this time, Kevin's uncle drew my attention to the link between his head and that of his nephew, Kevin; and then extended the link to the castle ruins. "Your uncle is showing me a link between the two of you and then to the castle."

As I said this, Kevin's uncle gave me the feeling of old times—times past. That, coupled with the fact that he showed me links between them and the castle ruins allowed me to ask Kevin this question: "Does it make sense to you that you and your uncle could have shared a lifetime in Ireland, perhaps even on the Dingle Peninsula and in or around that castle?"

"Interesting you should say that," said Kevin. "The feeling that I had been in that place before was so strong that I've started to explore the idea of reincarnation."

After the session ended, Kevin turned to me before walking out the door. "You know what's interesting? When my uncle died, he left money to me so I could take that trip. He used to talk to me about Ireland and said that he always wanted to go there for some reason. That's why I went."

Interesting indeed. As this encounter suggests, soul mates may be family members or others, with whom we've shared past lives.

I would like to emphasize that I do not consider myself a past-life regressionist (a person who helps others explore their past lives), nor do I consider myself an expert in reincarnation (the belief that each individual has lived many lives throughout history). For more information on the subject of reincarnation, I would direct you to the work of Brian Weiss, author of *Many Lives, Many Masters*.

The fact that we consider someone a soul mate doesn't avoid heartbreak. Sometimes soul-mate relationships are painful. This point was made exceptionally clear by a spirit named Philip, who was as handsome as a leading man yet left a path of destruction when he died.

"He was my soul mate," I heard Philip's fiancée, Julia, whisper as she started to sob into the phone. Up until this point, her voice had a stoic, flat tone to it. However, once she was convinced that I had a clear connection with Philip, it was as though her will to be strong crumbled. Philip stood before me in spirit, with a bad-boy's sly grin. Then I saw the gun and heard a bang.

"Yes, that's how he died—he shot himself," Julia said between sobs.

I paused to allow her to breathe and to see where Philip was going to lead the conversation. "Danny," he said.

I shared the name with Julia; and she knew exactly who Danny was and why he was important to Philip: "Danny gave Philip the drugs that were in his system the night he died. Danny was my dealer too," Julia confessed.

That was the last thing I expected Julia to say! And then I heard alarms, sirens, the piercing sound of the emergency broadcast system—all at the same time!

"Alarms, alarms!" I said to Julia. "They won't stop!"

And then she explained: the night Philip died, Julia heard sirens (which she later learned were headed to the scene of his suicide), then her house alarm went off for no apparent reason as a tornado-warning alert flashed across the TV screen. I understood the impact that all of these simultaneous alarms must have had.

Then I saw Philip smile that same bad-boy smile, I heard "wake-up call" and the name Mary. When I shared this phrase and name with Julia, she said, "I know, baby, I know." (I assumed that she was speaking to Philip, not to me.)

We sat there in silence for a moment and I felt my heart swelling with love as though it might burst.

What Julia went on to tell me was that when Philip died, neither of them knew that she was carrying his child. Brokenhearted, addicted, and pregnant, Julia accepted that the alarms and sirens the night of Philip's death were her wake-up call. She signed herself into rehab and ultimately gave birth to a girl she named Mary, who, despite the challenges around her inception, is a happy and healthy baby.

While speaking with Philip and Julia, I didn't see brackets—my symbol for deep connection that may last lifetimes. However, sometimes what I don't see, I feel with the heart. And that swelling of the heart tells me all I need to know. Mary, the baby that ties Philip and Julia together, may be a *living* link—a bracket, so to speak—with a baby's face.

What this encounter suggests is that a soul-mate connection, even a challenging one, may bring transformation and a dramatic change in life's direction and purpose. Some spiritual teachers today suggest that this kind of relationship is a "twin-flame relationship"—a deeply connected relationship, sometimes because of shared pain, that tends to be as tumultuous as it is harmonious, coming and going, and not always lasting a lifetime.

Yes, soul mates are a real thing, but the truth of who a soul mate can be to you is greater and more powerful than perhaps would be imagined in a "happily ever after" fairytale.

> *For more on the topic of relationships and connecting with your spirit guide, read chapter 5, "Afterlife Relationships."*

57. If my loved ones reincarnate before I die, will we miss seeing one another in the afterlife?

This question, asked at nearly every gallery event, expresses the fear that we may not only lose someone we love when they die but *again*, in the shuffle between Earth and the afterlife.

The frequency with which this question is asked is most likely a natural result of the growing acceptance of spirit communication and reincarnation in the Western world. Mediums and past-life researchers often teach at the same conferences; therefore, it shouldn't be surprising that conflation of the two (mediumship and past-life regression) has resulted in an intense anxiety that life is recycled and relationships are in flux. The situation is made worse by unskilled and misinformed mediums who assume that if they cannot connect with a sitter's loved one in spirit, that spirit must be back in another body somewhere on Earth! *Yikes!* Imagine making the assumption that when we attend a large party and don't get to see our friend Jeff, for example, that we then report to our friends, "Oh, Jeff must be dead; I didn't see him at the party." That would be ridiculous, right?

This misconception creates undue pain for people seeking help. For instance, a grieving mother came to me after being told at a reading that her son had been reincarnated as a drug-addicted pregnant woman living on the streets. This mother, hoping to find her grandchild, was driving through the streets of downtown Los Angeles trying to find her "son" and grandchild. *Double yikes!*

So how do we reconcile reunion with loved ones in spirit and reincarnation? Fortunately, my years working with spirits has yielded some answers. And as a medium with an international clientele, I've had the benefit of speaking with spirits of many different ethnic and religious backgrounds. Over time, I've noticed a couple of interesting consistencies. When I speak with people for whom reincarnation is a primary belief for many generations, spirits speak about reincarnation. When I speak with spirits in North America, the subject comes up with far less regularity.

With clients in India and Asia, reincarnation is nearly always a subject addressed within spirit messages. At first, I found this disconcerting, because reincarnation isn't my specialty. However, I am in service to spirits and am committed to providing messages *exactly* as I receive them—without editing, prejudice, or an overlay of my personal cultural background. So, I've persevered with willingness.

Sometimes this commitment is put to the test, like the time when I picked up the phone to speak with a client in India and the words, "Grandfather is here," popped out of my mouth.

Before I could see who said these words to me (I assumed it was the grandfather himself), the woman on the other end of the phone said, "Yes, that's right. He was born yesterday."

What??? I thought. The woman continued:

"My nephew, born yesterday morning, has two birthmarks—one on his arm and another on his ankle—in the exact same places as my grandfather. He also has the same eyes and eyebrows. We've named him Moti after his grandfather, and all the family agrees that it is Grandfather who has been born to be with us."

After this declaration by the sitter, it became clear that it was an uncle in spirit who was communicating with me. He had made the opening pronouncement and didn't correct his grandniece's opinion that his brother had been reborn. He did, however, discuss technology and how much he and his brother loved to keep pace with new innovations. Moti's aunt (or granddaughter, depending on how you look at it) confirmed that her grandfather used to say, "Computers will take over the world." Could it be that he chose to be born again to be part of that technological revolution? Perhaps.

Conversations like this don't happen often in the United States, which has caused me to ask the spirits "Why not?" during moments of contemplation. When I ask spirits to see what I'm not and understand what I don't, the answers are often revealed during a session. That's exactly what happened in the next case.

One bright May morning, I opened the door to my office to greet my next client. Standing there was a woman named Donna. She had spiky gray hair and was wearing a tie-dyed shirt, well-fitting designer jeans, and highly polished cowboy boots. She walked in with great confidence, sat down, and continued sipping her Starbucks coffee from a to-go cup.

As I cast my eyes around Donna, I caught sight of a blur, which signifies to me that I'm seeing a spirit who lived life in the fast lane. The spirit felt like a young male, but I heard the name "Ali," which could be for a boy or a girl. When I passed on this information, the woman nodded as though she understood. Then I saw a brick wall and felt as though I had slammed into it. The woman nodded at this information as well.

The session continued, and Ali had lots to say, but Donna said little in response. As Ali slowed down enough for me to catch a glimpse, I saw a great head of hair and heard in my ear the Richard Marx song "Right Here Waiting." When I started to sing the chorus, the lady set down her Starbucks cup, leaned back into the sofa, and began to cry. The young man in spirit stood very close to her, and it looked as though he was singing into her ear. I heard repeatedly, as though on loop, "I will be right here waiting for you."

Donna took a moment before speaking. I wasn't ready for what she had to say.

"We played that song at my son, Ali's, funeral," she explained. "It was always one of my favorite songs—actually, we both liked it. Ali even got his hair cut like Richard Marx." (No wonder I saw such great hair!) She continued, "When Ali got his license, I used to say to him, 'Drive carefully; I'll be right here waiting for you.' He hit a brick wall—literally—one night and died instantly. I was waiting at home that night when the police came to the door. I came here today with only one thing I wanted to know: Is Ali waiting for me now? Will I see my son again?"

Even as I sit here today thinking about this story, I feel a lump in my throat and a sting in my eyes. I even played a YouTube video of Richard Marx singing the song; it made me cry. It wasn't until Ali sang that song to his mother that I finally knew, without a doubt, that spirits wait for us. We will not—*cannot*—miss seeing our loved ones in spirit again one day.

After that session, I've heard the refrain of that song many times during sessions. It has become my reminder, and one I share with sitters, that yes, the one you love is waiting for you.

What spirits have inspired me to consider is this: In countries where the historical norm is reincarnation, sometimes, with barely a couple of generations between incarnations, a spirit who desires to experience multiple lives in quick succession will be born to believing families in those countries. However, people born in the United States and those who emigrate to this country seeking freedom to live a life of self-determination set the intention prior to incarnation to step off the karmic wheel and consequently break free from grief, pain, guilt, and all the baggage carried from lifetime to lifetime. In my experience with spirits, this has less to do with whether or not we, as Americans, believe in reincarnation. It has more to do with the ethos of freedom in our form of governance. I have witnessed a similar "migration" of souls to countries in Western Europe for much the same reason, I think.

The idea of spirits waiting might be difficult to grasp because much of the world lives according to linear time. For many of us, it is hard to believe that someone would hang around for five minutes, much less fifty years. You just have to be stuck on a line at the grocery store to understand that!

Clearly, spirits exist outside of time as we know it. The past, the present, and all future possibilities exist at the same time for them. This aspect of the afterlife is what allows a spirit to appear at an age they prefer; and why, sometimes, I'm not sure about whether an event has happened, is happening, or will be happening when spirits give me a message. From the perspective of spirits, "waiting" isn't an inactive state (they remain connected and involved in life on Earth), nor is there the perception of hours, days, weeks, months, and years going by. In other words, don't worry—they won't get tired of waiting for you and reincarnate just to avoid getting bored!

It is common for me to speak with fathers, grandfathers, and great-grandfathers during the same session. Their presence indicates that generations come together in the afterlife, reinforcing the idea that reincarnation may not simply be a revolving door between this life and the afterlife.

And finally, spirits provide reminders, through messages, that life isn't random; *love keeps us connected*. We don't need to go searching for spirits or for someone who may have reincarnated; we simply need to be still. Our bodies are our address on Earth—your spirits will find you. And when you no longer have a body, loved ones in spirit will be waiting.

> For more on intergenerational communication, read Q&A number 45, "Is it possible to communicate with our ancestors?" in chapter 6, "The Language of Spirits."

58. Is it possible to love again when you've lost everyone you love?

After losing someone we love, or *many* people that we love, it can be too painful to even contemplate being vulnerable again. I understand this to be true because I've experienced it. A man I loved dearly died suddenly in Paris—in the City of Love and Light. (The irony of that didn't escape me.) At the point of deepest despair, loneliness became my companion. This may surprise some because people assume that, as a medium, I am in touch with my loved ones in spirit 24/7. In fact, that isn't true. There's a bit of a catch-22 in being a medium. Because mediumship is a work of service, a "fail-safe" is built into the Universe to prevent abilities from being used solely for personal gain or for freedom from pain. Consequently, mediums experience grief much like everyone else.

As I worked my way through my grief, I was determined to keep my heart soft and open. And yes, I discovered love again, but only after being willing to invite it into my life, in a personal way. It was also during this time that I started working consistently at the frequency of love. Coincidence? I think not! What I do know, however, is that if *I* can invite love in again, you can too. What you may discover is that as you create space in your heart for earthly beings, you may find it easier to connect with loved ones in spirit as well.

It might seem counterintuitive to prepare for a new love relationship by practicing self-compassion and self-love. On the contrary, messages from loved ones in spirit often stress their concern for our welfare and well-being as an extension of their love for us. For example, a husband in spirit thanked his wife for taking care of him during a long illness. When his health started to rapidly decline, he died quickly thereafter. What he wanted his wife to know was that even his dying was an expression of his love for her. He had known that the care she provided was taking a physical and mental toll, so he decided to exit gracefully, before his illness destroyed her health too.

Upon hearing the message, his wife's face relaxed. She thought he had chosen to die because she wasn't doing *enough* to help keep him here! During the months following his death, she suffered from tremendous guilt; but in this moment of realization, a husband in spirit shifted a wife's self-blame into an extension of the love and compassion they had shared on Earth for twenty-seven years.

You don't have to wait for a message from spirits to release pain carried because of a loss or grief of another kind. No matter what you think may be separating you from love, here's an easy way to invite it in:

* Sit upright in a straight-backed chair, with your feet on the floor and your hands on your lap, palms facing up.

* Close your eyes.

* Think of someone you love. (If it is too painful to think of a person in spirit, think about a pet you currently have or a friend who has been supportive.)

* Allow the feeling of love to fill your chest and radiate outward.

* Imagine that the person you're thinking of is receiving your love, that they are surrounded by it, that they are filled with it.

* Sitting quietly, with your eyes closed, imagine that the person or pet you love is sitting on a chair directly opposite you.

* Just as you offered them love, they now offer love to you.

* Accept their love, allowing it to fill your heart.

* Sit with this feeling for as long as it is comfortable for you.

At first, it may be easier to receive love from someone you love rather than loving yourself. I've certainly found this to be true in my own life. Fortunately, this exercise can be adapted to allow yourself the freedom to accept yourself and even the parts of yourself that you've judged to be unlovable: simply visualize your own face as a child rather than the face of a loved one in spirit. As you extend love to the child you were (and still are) and draw that love back into your heart, allow yourself to rest in the release and peace it brings. Personally, I've used this exercise to love my young "stocky" self (a phrase that my grandmother used to describe my body type), which has helped to bring healing to painful memories of being an over-weight kid.

As I've learned self-love and have practiced self-compassion, in turn, I've allowed others to love me (since it now doesn't seem like such an onerous task)! Once love is invited in, we can remain connected to the love of spirits and the love of ourselves by expressing compassion and unconditional love to those on Earth.

The masters of this kind of generous, no-strings-attached life are pets on Earth and in spirit. For example, at a public event some time ago, a spirit shared with a couple in the audience that their beloved Labrador would be joining the spirit world. Although spirits don't predict death during readings, it was clear that they wanted the couple to know that when the time came, all would be well; and they would be guided to another loving Labrador retriever. This same couple attended a later event, and afterward, gave me a photo of their new, gorgeous Lab named (and I'm not kidding) Hollister Rand Lewis! Rest assured that the pets (and the people) we love in spirit know that they cannot be replaced; but they also know that their love for us can be expressed through others we've invited into our lives.

If you're missing a beloved pet, get involved by volunteering at or donating blankets, food, and so forth to shelters and rescues, which can help you feel connected. To experience the direct action of spirits, you may consider a more hands-on approach, such as helping at a rescue event. At such events, I have seen pets in spirit matching the families they love with another loving bundle of fur. Pets in spirit can even impress prospective pets on Earth to act like them (which certainly catches the future owner's attention).

Love for family members in spirit can be shown by helping others in ways that your loved ones in spirit would appreciate. For instance, my mother was a teacher, librarian, and lover of books. I wasn't surprised, therefore, when a library in Long Beach, California, asked if I would donate my time for a fundraiser (which, of course, I did). During the event, I shared messages from loved ones in spirit while knowing that my mother was with me. Together, we shared our love of learning and books with many who would benefit from the library's work.

If the one you love enjoyed family gatherings, organize one (for no apparent reason). If your loved one was a sports fanatic, donate a pair of tickets for a home game to a worthy cause. If your loved one enjoyed reading, consider volunteering at a literacy organization. If your loved one was open and friendly, smile at a stranger.

59. Are spirits aware of disasters, including ecological ones?

During events and sessions, loved ones in spirit will often mention earthly events—an upcoming wedding, a son going off to war, or a memorial fundraiser for an overseas orphanage. It seems obvious that loved ones in spirit would be interested and connected to events such as these.

However, the interest of those in the afterlife extends well beyond their own families. When I've spoken with spirits who have died in tsunamis, earthquakes, bombings, and plane crashes, there is often a reference to helping other people who pass in the same way. For example, a Navy man in spirit, who died during World War II, told me that one of the ways he helps is as a spirit "first responder" when disasters at sea occur. When I boarded my first cruise last year, I thought of this man and thanked him (not that I was expecting our ship to sink, of course). The idea of spirit first responders is of great comfort to me as I move through this uncertain world.

So, what do spirits do in response to a disaster? Spirits inspire people on Earth who are willing to create solutions. Sometimes the people chosen are unlikely heroes, like a movie star or a chef. It seems as though the more unlikely the hero, the greater the spirit inspiration behind his or her actions!

As overwhelming and heartbreaking as a disaster may be, it is also an opportunity for the love of those who have passed to be expressed to those left behind. For example, if a child becomes an orphan in an earthquake in Haiti, the desire of a US couple to adopt that child may be at the prompting of his parents in spirit. When disaster strikes, whether natural or human-made, spirits are ready to respond.

Now, just because spirits are ready, doesn't mean that *we* don't have to be. Efforts during disastrous times are cooperative between people on Earth and people in spirit. The concern and care that spirits extend to Earth is frequently transmuted into a call for strangers to help— whether or not communication with spirits is acknowledged. In the aftermath of the recent hurricanes, people from around the world were moved to dedicate time and money. Because of that disaster, US citizens, including me, are now aware of the poverty of Puerto Rico and the support its people need. As I walked through the streets of San Juan, I could sense that spirits were working behind the scenes.

Spirits often talk with me about personal responsibility, as there are no rationalizations in the afterlife. When something like an oil spill or leak wreaks havoc on the environment and threatens wildlife, *every person* on the planet is ultimately affected. Consequently, in the larger sense, we're *all* responsible for Earth's well-being, to one degree or another. From spirits' points of view, the interconnectedness of all life is apparent.

Those in spirit have experienced the transformation we call death, so it makes sense that they would help to guide us through sudden changes here on Earth. Every disaster is an opportunity to step beyond blame and make a difference through personal responsibility. Every disaster is a profound call to action to express the love and compassion of the spirit world in the world we share on Earth.

Change and transformation, love and compassion—this is the way of spirits, and it can be ours as well, during days of disaster and every day.

For more insight on ghosts and spirits, read Q&A number 3, "Is there a difference between a ghost and a spirit?" in chapter 1, "The Basics."

60. Can spirits help change my destiny?

"He was *never* supposed to die!" the woman on the phone said to me.

This statement was in response to her husband in spirit giving me a sudden pain in my chest to indicate a heart attack, after which a photo of a Hawaiian cruise was flashed into my mind. The distraught woman on the phone acknowledged that she had planned a cruise to celebrate her husband's retirement. What she hadn't planned for was that, on the day he retired, her husband would die of a massive heart attack.

Years before, on their wedding day, she had decided that they would live happily ever after, and the phrase "till death do us part" had been purposefully left out of their vows—the story of their lives together didn't have an ending as far as she was concerned. So, when death suddenly interrupted the story that she had lived by, it made her extremely angry. In the story, she told herself her husband was *never* supposed to die.

While reading this, you may scratch your head and wonder how someone could overlook such an obvious fact of life. And yet, time after time, messages from spirits ask that we reconsider the stories we tell about ourselves and the deaths of those we miss so desperately. We all choose to overlook the possibility that someone we love may die in a way or at a time that is completely unacceptable to us. At a book signing, a woman with desperate eyes told me, "My son killed himself on my birthday. How could that happen? What does it mean?" I've come to discover that one of my greatest responsibilities as a medium is to give spirits opportunities to revise and rewrite the stories of their lives, and cocreate new storylines with their loved ones living on Earth.

These new storylines often begin with two words: "I'm sorry." Spirits have often reported to me that after dying, they were able to view their lives without the benefit of any rationalizations or excuses; they could literally experience the ramifications of their own actions, both positive and negative. This broadened awareness allows those in spirit to interact with us in ways that can be different from—and better than—the ways they chose while in the physical body.

Change, as we all know, is the only constant in life and death (and that's actually the good news). In my experience, spirits exhibit enthusiasm for change. For example, during a phone session, a brilliant inventor and father in spirit apologized to his daughter for disapproving of her creative pursuits as a young girl. As a result of her father's discouragement, and in an effort to please him, she became a doctor instead of an actress. However, as her father readily acknowledged during the session, he now recognizes how his own fears in life limited the self-expression of his daughter. During the session, he declared himself an ally in her creative projects and supported that fact with a number of specific references made regarding the theatrical plays that she hopes to bring to the public.

One of the things I love the most about my work is witnessing how spirits inspire us to rewrite our own stories and cocreate with them a new way of living. A mother in spirit expressed tremendous concern about her son, who had been recently diagnosed with diabetes.

"I never took care of my blood sugar," she confessed. She also stressed that her son didn't have to suffer as she did, which included losing part of a leg and going blind toward the end of her life.

Her son was shocked when his mother in spirit reported a conversation that he had had with another family member almost word for word. "Yeah, I'm going to go the way my mom did. Nothin' much I can do about it," he had stated. Well, his mother disagreed with him and made it clear that she would provide signs of encouragement on the path to his wellness. Her son has now lost almost thirty pounds and may very well avoid suffering through to the end—the story he used to relate.

Spirits may help us to rewrite what we tell ourselves (and others) about their deaths. When a sister in spirit who had died in her early twenties came to visit during a session, she made it clear that she literally "didn't see it coming." She then went on to describe the head-on collision that ended her life. This was a tremendous relief to the sister she had left behind, who had lived for many years with the fear that her sister's last moments on Earth were terrifying. The younger sister in spirit went on to say that she was watching over her sister and all of those she loves. In one masterful stroke, the younger sister in spirit changed the story of "my sister died alone and terrified" to "my sister loves me, and watches over me and those I love." What a difference!

The freeing, healing, and empowering messages of hope from loved ones in spirit raise questions about what we hold on to as "the way things are." Spirits support the grain of truth in each story, but they also ask us to reconsider the interpretations we've added on and the endings that we assume are foregone conclusions. The way spirits tell it, the stories of our lives are new beginnings in the making; and they want to help us discover those new beginnings.

For the wife whose husband died before they could enjoy retirement together, their story together hasn't ended, as she so wanted to believe. For the daughter whose father discouraged her from having a career in the theater, her dreams are there for the taking, with the knowledge that her father stands with her and applauds her accomplishments. For the big sister who thought her younger sister died in fear, fear can be left behind, because she knows she is protected by her sister in spirit. For the son who thought he had no choice but to suffer illness as his mother did, a healthier life is now a reality.

I feel prompted to end this answer with the question "What is your story?" Whatever the answer is, I know that your loved ones in spirit are ready, willing, and able to help you change it for the better.

> For more on the topic of spirit influence, read Q&A number 34, "Can spirits intervene on our behalf?" in chapter 5, "Afterlife Relationships."

61. Can we escape our karma?

While visiting Thailand, I came across a pamphlet written in English about karma. One of the practices suggested for transmuting karma was to give alms to a monk. Consequently, during my trip, I gave alms to anyone who even looked like a monk! However, since I wasn't going to be staying in Thailand and I wasn't within reach of a monk each day, I spent some time thinking about other ways to lighten my karmic load.

Although my daily interaction with monks is minimal, I *do* have a huge amount of experience listening to spirits speak about life. Over time, I've become aware of thematic refrains when it comes to spirit messages. One of these recurring refrains is the insistence that, ultimately, everyone is responsible for his or her actions. Personal responsibility is the hue and cry of spirits—no matter their religious background on Earth.

Karma, the cosmic law of cause and effect, is the great teacher of personal responsibility. The wheel of karma allows these opportunities to come around and around again until we have the aha moment that prompts the desire to change. Oftentimes, death itself provides the opportunity for that aha moment because addictions and all other physical afflictions pass away. And over the years, spirits have shown me these four steps we can take to get out of the way of the wheel of karma *before* it runs us over.

First, be aware.

Listen to what you say about life in general and about your life in particular. Pay attention to using words like *always* and *never* when describing experiences. For instance, during a session with a young woman, her father in spirit apologized for abandoning the family when she was two. He admitted that her current relationship difficulties were related to his choice. "Yeah," the girl agreed. "Men always do a disappearing act. My boyfriend is never around." Loved ones in spirit are quick to point out that the polarized way we view life is often the result of their teaching us that life is one way or another.

The idea of "that's just the way life is" can be accepted so early in our existence that it is difficult to consider that what we assume is "truth" may *not* be—especially when personal experience supports our claims. The young woman's father in spirit reminded her that her best friend, Sarah, is happily married with a baby. In talking about Sarah, she had an aha moment: "Maybe all men *aren't* the same," she said as she walked out the door.

Second, be present.

One of the challenges I face when communicating with spirits is ascertaining whether they are referring to past, present, or future events and actions. The reason for this is that spirits almost always provide information in the present tense. For example, during a recent session, a husband in spirit who had left behind a wife and young children, mentioned Hawaii. At the same time, he showed me a beach in my mind that gave me the sense he was with his family in Hawaii and felt at home on the Big Island. It turns out that the man had lived in Hawaii before he had gotten married (past), that his family had scattered his ashes on the beach in Hawaii (present, because they were in Hawaii when the session had been scheduled), and that there were plans of returning to Hawaii regularly (future). The past, present, and future existed simultaneously in the present for this loving husband and father.

The fact that spirits live in the present is helpful when thinking about change in our own lives. To make everlasting change, it is essential to work from exactly where we are. The past and future can only be affected by what we do in the present moment. When paying attention to things as they are *right now*, we are no longer locked into a rote way of living and are free to question whether what we believe about life is true. Make it a practice to live as spirits live—in the present tense.

Third, be willing.

One of the greatest misconceptions we maintain about spirits is that they are fixed in their ways and that change is impossible after death. This couldn't be further from the truth. For instance, a father in spirit who had ostracized his son for being gay made it clear during a session that he had not only changed his mind but also admired his son for his strength and activism.

Fourth, be grateful.

Spirits almost always express gratitude for the ways that we've honored and loved them while they were on Earth and after their death. "Thank you for helping me keep my dignity," a mother in spirit told the daughter who had bathed her day after day so that she wouldn't be naked in front of a stranger. "Thank you for your friendship and encouragement," a group of children and teenagers in spirit told a young woman who was fighting the cancer from which many of them had died. Gratitude has been severely underrated, and spirits remind us to elevate it to its rightful (and helpful) place in creating everlasting change.

✳ ✳ ✳

Be Aware. Be Present. Be Willing. Be Grateful. These four simple steps can be life (and life after life after life) changing.

62. Can spirits help us find peace after loss?

Inner quiet and tranquility can be disrupted by loss (outer conflict) and what we tell ourselves about that loss (inner conflict). Whether the loss of personal peace is the result of the death of a family member, a change in our financial situation, or painful divorce proceedings, a sense of inner peace may seem to be lost forever to turmoil. However, this need not be the case, as spirits reassure again and again. Spirits have much to say about peace.

When people ask me whether a loved one in spirit is "happy," the spirit's response is almost always to give me a sense of abiding peace. As a medium, I'm privileged to actually *feel* this peace; and when I'm in that space, my only thought is, *I want more of this!*

How can we access and own the peace that spirits speak about? For starters, it is important to see things from the spirits' perspective—and be willing to let go of whatever stands in the way of personal peace. If you're ready to restore or create inner peace, here are some ways to do so.

Acknowledge the current situation and be willing to sit with your feelings, even if they're uncomfortable.

When I speak with spirits, they are up-front and honest about their words and deeds while living on Earth, especially if their actions painfully affected others. Spirits readily express remorse, gratitude, and love. It always surprises me when a spirit who died by suicide is shocked that his or her death was hard for others. In honestly addressing actions and feelings, and taking personal responsibility for both, the pathway to peace begins.

Bring love and self-compassion into the process of inviting peace.

One of the reasons that spirits are able to confront their lives honestly is because their life review is presented in the supportive embrace of love. Most of us are much harder on ourselves than we are on others. When castigating yourself about a perceived failure, talk to yourself as you would a dear friend or family member that you love. Tell yourself what your heart needs to hear for healing.

Let go of a limited concept of justice.

One of the challenges to maintaining inner peace is living in a world where justice is rarely (if ever) "perfect" and often seems nonexistent. The injustice of being overlooked for a promotion, or a loved one dying due to murder or negligence, can cause sleepless nights and drive us to unhealthy ways of coping. In situations where things are just plain wrong, spirits remind us of two things: (1) our love for others (as well as ourselves) isn't proven by the justice we earn for them, and (2) no one gets away with anything in the end. There *is* perfect justice in the afterlife—all is brought into balance and all is understood. Releasing the idea that justice must be served in exactly the way you think it should be allows the perfect and divine justice of the Universe to prevail—and *it will.*

Enlist practices to physically calm yourself.

Spirits remember what it is like to live in a physical body. For example, a message from a husband in spirit celebrated the fact that his former wife had found a new partner—he didn't want her to live life alone, without the support and companionship of another person. Spirits share memories of family meals, of celebrating holidays, and of physical pain they experienced on the Earth plane. Therefore, when spirits talk about ways to care for and calm our physical selves, it is important to take notice. Pets in spirit often convey that they are making their presence known by jumping on a bed, influencing another pet in the household, or hiding toys. These spirit animals remind us that the simple act of petting a dog or a cat, listening to purring, or playing fetch can calm the nervous system, helping to create a physical sense of inner peace.

A grandmother in spirit recently ordered her granddaughter to "get out my tea set and make tea like we used to do." Perhaps a cup of herbal tea or another kind of warm beverage is in order when you're stressed. And if you drink out of a cup belonging to a loved one in spirit, all the better!

Spirits remember the power of human touch to bring healing. During sessions with a spirit who is a hugger, I tingle from my head to my toes. When a young man in spirit mentioned that his mom wears his leather jacket, he exclaimed to her with delight, "When you wear it, I'm hugging you!" Loved ones in spirit can also inspire *others* to give you a hug! Getting a massage or even rubbing your own upper arms can calm the nervous system. Restoring inner peace may be as simple as allowing touch back into your life.

Be willing to live in connection with loved ones on Earth and in spirit.

When we commit to living in connection, we're able to access the eternal peace that spirits speak about. Living in connection reminds us that we are part of a bigger whole, and that *everyone* and *everything* has purpose. Many people seem to think that inner peace is only possible when we "get away from it all"; spirits present a different concept: peace is only possible *in the midst of it all.* So today, make time to call a friend, read a book about spirit communication, attend a medium's event, or take a class to expand your awareness of spirits.

* * *

On a daily basis, we are hit with things that can rob us of our inner peace. However, by remaining connected and acting in loving ways toward oneself and others, the path to inner peace can be restored.

Conclusion

> It is by logic that we prove but by intuition that we discover.

Henri Poincaré,
French mathematician,
theoretical physicist,
and engineer

As the book comes to an end, I hope that it has been a helpful start to understanding the world of spirits or an encouraging next step on a journey that has already begun.

The answers shared in this book have several things in common:

* They support the idea that consciousness survives death.

* They provide an understanding that relationships continue beyond death.

* They encourage getting connected and staying connected to those we love in spirit, so that we can be guided, comforted, and healed.

While writing this book, I was constantly challenged by my excellent editing team to explain things simply and clearly. What I realized is that I take a lot for granted because of my years of experience with spirits. Writing this book has been humbling, as it reminded me of why I do this work in the first place—for those "left behind." For most people, the first time they even think about spirit communication is after the loss of someone they love. Indeed, grief may feel like a locked door between this world and the afterlife, but I'm hoping that within these pages, you have found one key to opening that door.

One of the greatest challenges of writing this book was deciding which questions to include from the many questions that have been asked during the twenty-five years of my career as a medium. In fact, as I type these final words, I can't help but think, *There's so much more to share!* Therefore, this isn't really "the end"; as spirits have made clear to me, there isn't an end, even when, as in death, it looks like one.

My work and I are accessible to you. I am a working and teaching medium who answers questions on Facebook and posts photos on Instagram; and I will be continuing to answer questions online, in my newsletter (sign up at HollisterRand.com), in magazines, and at events.

Remember to stay curious and keep asking questions. The spirits are ready to answer!

The End
(Not really)

If you want to find the secrets of the universe, think in terms of energy, frequency, and vibration.

Nikola Tesla

Acknowledgments

Thanks to . . .

Carole Bozzi—for keeping my rear in gear;

Michele and Richard Cohn—for believing in the book;

Carlos Cordova—for being my Prints Charm'n;

Rich Devin—for making me feel at home in Las Vegas;

Emily Han—for editing my natural volubility, and challenging me to
be clear and concise;

Tom Laurie—for loving me always;

Michelle Lynskey—for being a friend for all seasons;

Anthony May and Tim Jones—for becoming family;

Danielle MacKinnon—for being my heart sister;

Mary Anne Pusey—for great moments and memories at the beach;

Bodhi and Amara Rand—for being the loves of my life;

Wendy Rettig—for being the best sister I have;

Barry Shulman—for being my champion;

Carolyn Surtees—for sharing your love and your wardrobe;

Lance Taubold—for remembering when we were young;

Angela Tiseo—for the laughs throughout the years;

Savannah van der Keyl—for your positive attitude, no matter the task;

Jane WeMett—for not only being a beloved aunt but also a friend;

Sara Wiseman—for causing me to think with my heart.

Appendix: Q&A Cross-References

Q&A	Related Q&A(s)
1. Is there really an afterlife?	2
2. Do spirits tell you what the afterlife is like?	1
3. Is there a difference between a ghost and a spirit?	10, 59
5. What is mediumship for?	30
7. Do all spirits communicate with mediums in the same way?	36, 37
8. Can mediums communicate with spirits who speak a different language?	45
10. Do you ever receive messages that you don't feel comfortable communicating?	3
11. Do religious figures such as Mother Mary and Jesus communicate through mediums?	52
17. If I don't get to say goodbye before I die, is it too late to do so after?	30
21. What happens to people who commit suicide?	55
25. Are there seasons/climates in the afterlife?	Chapter 8

30. Do spirits know how much we love and miss them?	5, 17
33. Do spirits get jealous?	56
34. Can spirits intervene on our behalf?	60
36. What is the difference between guides and angels?	7, 37, 48, 53
37. How can I meet my spirit guide?	7, 36
42. Do spirits come to us as insects and animals?	Chapter 7
45. Is it possible to communicate with our ancestors?	8, 57
48. Do animals in spirit help us in our lives?	36
52. Do spirits tell you if there's a God?	11
53. What does it mean to be spiritually connected?	36
55. Do spirits agree with us about what is good and what is bad?	21
56. Are soul mates a real thing?	33, Chapter 5
57. If my loved ones reincarnate before I die, will we miss seeing one another in the afterlife?	45
59. Are spirits aware of disasters, including ecological ones?	3
60. Can spirits help change my destiny?	34

Notes

1. Caryle Murphy, "Most Americans Believe in Heaven . . . and Hell," *Fact Tank: News in the Numbers*, Pew Research Center, November 10, 2015, https://www.pewresearch.org/fact-tank/2015/11/10/most-americans-believe-in-heaven-and-hell/.

2. Gail Hairston, "US May Have More Atheists Than Previously Assumed," *University of Kentucky News*, May 25, 2017, https://uknow.uky.edu/research/us-may-have-more-atheists-previously-assumed.

3. Wendy Daniels-Virstra, "What a beautiful experience, Hollister," May 26, 2019, comment on Medium Hollister Rand, "Dear friends, I'm so excited to be traveling to the Huntington Beach New Earth Expo today," https://www.facebook.com/HollisterRand/posts/10156626946694582.

4. Anna Marie January, "I am one of the Annas. (We sat next to each other, even though we didn't know each other.) You talked to both of us." Facebook, January 14, 2018, https://www.facebook.com/HollisterRand/photos/a.307319319581/10155492534294582/?type=3&theater.

5. Anna Bäck, LAc, "I am the "other" Aanna, the one with the hummingbird tattoo. I originally sat several rows back and, at the last minute, decided to move up." Facebook, January 14, 2018, https://www.facebook.com/HollisterRand/photos/a.307319319581/10155492534294582/?type=3&theater.

6. Nicci French, *Day of the Dead: A Novel* (A Frieda Klein Novel) (New York, NY: William Morrow Paperbacks, 2018), 403.

7. "The Water in You: Water and the Human Body," USGS Water Science School, accessed August 18, 2019, https://www.usgs.gov/special-topic /water-science-school/science/water-you-water-and-human-body?qt -science_center_objects=0#qt-science_center_objects.

8. Larry Shannon-Missal, "More Than Ever, Pets Are Part of the Family," *The Harris Poll* #41 (July 16, 2015): https://theharrispoll.com /whether-furry-feathered-or-flippers-a-flapping-americans-continue -to-display-close-relationships-with-their-pets-2015-is-expected-to -continue-the-pet-industrys-more-than-two-decades-strong/.

Recommended Resources

Books

Alexander, Eben. *Proof of Heaven: A Neurosurgeon's Journey into the Afterlife*. New York: Simon & Schuster, 2012.

Bulkeley, Kelly. *Big Dreams: The Science of Dreaming and the Origins of Religion*. Oxford, England: Oxford University Press, 2016.

Farmer, Steven D. *Healing Ancestral Karma: Free Yourself from Unhealthy Family Patterns*. San Antonio, TX: Hierophant Publishing, 2014.

Farmer, Steven D. *Power Animals: How to Connect with Your Animal Spirit Guide*. Carlsbad, CA: Hay House, 2004.

Farmer, Steven D. *Spirit Animals: As Guides, Teachers, and Healers*. East Lismore, New South Wales: Animal Dreaming Publishing, 2017.

MacKinnon, Danielle. *Animal Lessons: Discovering Your Spiritual Connection with Animals*. Woodbury, MN: Llewellyn Publications, 2017.

Moorjani, Anita. *Dying to Be Me: My Journey from Cancer, to Near Death, to True Healing*. Carlsbad, CA: Hay House, 2012.

Warraich, Haider. *Modern Death: How Medicine Changed the End of Life.* New York: St. Martin's Griffin, 2018.

Weiss, Brian L. *Many Lives, Many Masters: The True Story of a Prominent Psychiatrist, His Young Patient, and the Past-Life Therapy That Changed Both Their Lives.* New York: Fireside, 1988.

Wiseman, Sara. *The Intuitive Path: The Seeker's Guide to Spiritual Intuition.* Scotts Valley, CA: CreateSpace, 2012.

Wiseman, Sara. *Messages from the Divine: Wisdom for the Seeker's Soul.* Hillsboro, OR: Beyond Words / Atria Books, 2018.

Organizations

Edgar Cayce's Association for Research and Enlightenment (ARE)
EdgarCayce.org

Provides resources to explore meditation, intuition, dream interpretation, prayer, holistic health, ancient mysteries, and philosophical concepts such as karma, reincarnation, and the meaning of life.

International Association for Near-Death Studies (IANDS)
IANDS.org

IANDS is dedicated to creating a greater awareness and understanding of near-death and other related experiences through research, education, and support.

Lily Dale Assembly
LilyDaleAssembly.org

Lily Dale Assembly is the world's largest center for the Religion of
Spiritualism, and its purpose is to further the science and philosophy of the religion.

Spiritualist Church of the Comforter
scotc.org

This loving congregation is committed to the Principles of Spiritualism and provides a welcoming presence for people and spirits in
beautiful Santa Barbara, CA.

About the Author

During the last twenty-five years, Hollister Rand's dedication to the healing work of mediumship has included events and workshops in the United States and abroad. And it has been her honor to work with other respected mediums, including Robert Brown and John Edward.

Hollister's work on television shows includes *Tori & Dean: Home Sweet Hollywood* and *America Now*. Her radio appearances include SiriusXM's "The Séance with John Edward" (on *John Edward Psychic Radio*), KOST FM's *Angels in Waiting*, KBIG FM's *Radio Medium*, and *Coast to Coast with George Noory*.

Hollister's first book, *I'm Not Dead, I'm Different: Kids in Spirit Teach Us about Living a Better Life on Earth*, published by Harper-Collins, is available in several languages.

Hollister lives in Los Angeles with her impossibly small chihuahuas, Bodhi and Amara Metta.

Visit her at HollisterRand.com.

A biographical footnote from Hollister Rand

Along with all the questions in this book, there's one other that is asked with increasing frequency at events. Even so, I was surprised when a woman raised her hand and asked in front of a room of workshop participants, "Were you married to James Van Praagh?"

The answer to that question is yes.